CATHOLICISM IN A NUTSHELL

By Steven Speray

VERITAS

DEFENDING THE HISTORIC CATHOLIC CHURCH

Catholicism in a Nutshell

Second Edition

Copyright 2009 by Steven Speray

ISBN: 978-0-578-04900-7

Published by Confiteor
P.O. Box 83
Versailles, KY 40383
www.catholictopgun.com

Introduction

The following writings were a series of letters and essays I used to explain and defend the Catholic faith to family, friends and co-workers.

Each time a question would come up; I would sit down and write out a little explanation and defense of each doctrine.

I always felt that putting it down on paper in a simple and short letter or essay would help individuals see the logic of the arguments always having a reference for what is stated. It also helps me not to repeat myself over and over by word of mouth.

It seems that most people don't like to read long and drawn out explanations. By keeping the essay particularly short, I could hammer down on the main points and without losing the interest of the reader.

The letters have been slightly modified from the originals to better fit the short essay format of this book.

What you see is basically still raw and unedited.

My training was in strategic weapons systems of the US Navy. I took up writing in responding to opinions in the local paper. Later, I used writing as a way to engage in religious debates.

With the thirteen listed essays, all the main objections to Catholicism are defended and explained. Of course, many more objections can be listed, but the same logic used in these thirteen can be applied to all the rest.

Also included within the essays are very brief arguments, reasons or implications why not to believe in popular heresies such as: The Rapture, Bible Alone, Faith Alone, Invisible Church, Eternal Security, Irresistible Grace, Limited Atonement, etc.

The last essay is a bonus.

This Second Edition has a changed font with a few typo fixes.

TABLE OF CONTENTS

All Scripture quotes come from one of the following sources:
    Douay-Rheims, Confraternity (Challoner Rheims), Revised
    Standard Version Catholic Edition

1. Arguments for the Existence of God in a Nutshell

The following arguments will be given in no particular order.

First, there is absolutely no evidence against the existence of God. While this is a negative argument, nevertheless, evidence for the existence of God can be found in logic and reason with the use of historical events.

Documented miracles attest to the existence of God. A miracle is an event that was caused outside the laws of nature. It is not a mere oddity or an extremely unusual happening.

An example of a miracle would be a raising of the dead. Near death experience or a starting of one's heart through scientific means would not qualify as a raising of the dead. However, one who has been dead for days or years already deteriorating or completely deteriorated and rose by the power of Christ's name would definitely qualify as a miracle and such cases are in existence.

The miracle of Lanciano is on-going miracle that is completely against the laws of nature. Living tissue and blood with all the properties of living blood in an uncontrolled environment that is over 1300 years old cannot be explained by any natural or scientific method. This miracle involving a sacrament of the Roman Catholic Church corresponds to the one God of Christians is strong evidence for the existence of God.

Many more examples of miracles can be given but this suffices.

The argument of causality is another example of evidence proving the existence of God.

All things are caused but the initial cause must itself be uncaused. This Uncaused Cause is God.

Nothing cannot cause something into being. Nothing can only produce nothingness. Life itself comes from life. Life doesn't come out of non-life. Therefore, all life must ultimately be caused by that which is Life itself. This Life being we call God must have existed eternally which is outside of time.

It is illogical to say that all causes come from an endless series of causes and no uncaused caused is necessary. It would mean that the present time of all things are simultaneously the cause and effect of each other. This is absurd. The present now is dependent upon a cause now, which must be outside of time.

From the argument of cause and effect we get the argument of change as evidence for God. If God exists outside of space and time then God must cause space and time.

Matter in space and time changes but it cannot change without a cause. The material universe is the sum of all matter, space, and time. If nothing exists outside of the material universe, then the matter, space, and time cannot change since all of these elements are dependent upon each other. Something must exist outside of the material universe to cause matter, space, and time to change or else it would never change, nor could it even have a potential to change.

The argument of perfection is also good evidence for the existence of God.

We all recognize that some things are better than others, and the degrees of being have levels of goodness. Therefore, we recognize the superiority of all the different ways of being. The level or degree of perfection is the standard by which all degrees and levels are measured. If degrees of perfection pertain to being then the ultimate level and perfect being would be God.

Other arguments used to give evidence for the existence of God are the order of the universe and consciousness. However, the most controversial and the most philosophical argument for the existence of God is the Ontological Argument. It was devised by Anselm of Canterbury (1033-1109) as the simplest explanation for God's existence. It is far from simple. It is so profound that non-thinkers dismiss it as a riddle. Some philosophers find it quite interesting.

In brief, it goes like this: It is greater for something to exist in thought and in reality rather in thought only. Since God is that which a greater cannot be thought then in reality He must exist because it would be impossible to have the thought of a greater than God.

Lastly, men can look at any object and can tell that either nature or man made it. How can one look at the universe as a whole including life and dismiss its cause as not existing? Is this not the ultimate absurdity?

There is no such thing as an invincibly ignorant atheist. (Romans 1:18-21)

2. Reasons to believe that Jesus is God in a Nutshell

It is a historical fact that a man named Jesus from a town called Nazareth existed.

Whether or not he is God is the question.

What reasons would there be to believe Jesus is God?

It is an interesting question since most Christians take it for granted.

Why should a non-Christian, such as a Jew or Buddhist, believe it?

On the subjective level, this famous quote applies to the question, *"For those who believe, no explanation is needed, for those who don't believe, no explanation is possible."*

Objectively speaking however, reasons can be given that may help one to accept such a belief in Jesus.

Before looking at the given reasons, Jews should consider the prophecies concerning the Messiah, such as (Psalm 22, Isaiah 9:6-7), and especially (Isaiah 53). Jesus fulfills all the prophecies of Holy Scripture concerning the Messiah. With this in mind, note the following evidence in conjunction with the above prophecies.

Interestingly, the founder of Buddhism, Siddhartha Gautama, predicted that 500 years after him that God would come into the world as a man. Jesus came about 500 years after Gautama. Buddhists should take careful note of the following.

Perhaps the best reason for believing that Jesus is God is the historical testimony and witness of his immediate followers especially the Apostles themselves.

Nearly all of them died horrific deaths for claiming that Jesus had resurrected from the dead proving He was who He said He was.

Now it is not surprising to see people giving up their lives for something they believe in.

Even today, some groups of Muslims proudly die expecting to receive the rewards promised them in their Koran.

However, this is entirely different from giving up one's life in a horrific fashion for something he claims to have seen and heard.

The Apostles believed it because they said they witnessed it.

If it were a lie, they would simply retract what they said and live.

Yet, they didn't do so.

All were willing to go to death for it.

People don't voluntarily die painful deaths for something they know to be a lie.

St. Paul didn't even witness it.

At first being an anti-Christian putting Christians to death, he claims to hear Christ's voice questioning him after being struck down with a strange temporary blindness as he traveled to Damascus.

Afterwards, St. Paul believed to the point of traveling around the known world surviving several shipwrecks, enduring extreme hardships such as many physical beatings, several imprisonments, and ultimately death by beheading.

He is truly a powerful witness.

One could argue that he went mad as his conscience got the better of him for killing Christians.

But then again, you have the rest of the Apostles.

All of them were at first terrified of being persecuted for following and believing in Jesus after He died.

After the Resurrection and Descent of the Holy Ghost, all of them traveled quite extensively spreading the Gospel also enduring many hardships.

They all based their new Faith on Christ's Resurrection, which they all claim that Jesus spent 40 days on earth after He rose from the dead, eating, drinking, and teaching them. St. Thomas doubted and was instructed by Jesus to put his hands into the nail marks and believe.

After the 40 days, they claim to watch Him ascend into Heaven.

In the end...

St. Peter ultimately was murdered upside down on a cross as he wished in 64 or 67 AD. He didn't feel worthy of dying as His Lord.

In 69 AD, his brother, St. Andrew, was murdered on a cross in the form of an "X" and then converted 2000 people talking about Christ as he hung on his cross.

St. James the Greater was the first Apostle to die by being beheaded in 47 AD.

His brother St. John died naturally of old age from a crippling illness but once was boiled in oil and lived to tell about it.

St. Philip was 87 years old when he was also crucified upside down.

St. Bartholomew was skinned alive and crucified on Aug 4, 62 AD.

St. James the Less was stoned to death in 62 AD at 60 years of age.

St. Matthew died around 90 AD and his is the only death that is unknown.

St. Thomas died July 3, 72 AD from Impalement (speared).

St. Simon and St. Jude Thaddeus died together in 79 AD: Simon by being sawed into pieces and Jude from impalement.

St. Matthias was murdered in 51 AD by stoning.

That adds up to a most impressive witness giving the world a strong reason to believe in Christ's Resurrection as an historical fact.

Thus, this fact denotes that Jesus was God.

Now using the Bible as merely a historical record, we see different authors tell us that Jesus saying or implying that He is God.

As a matter of fact, Jesus was crucified for saying so.

One may argue that Christ says that He is only the Son of God, which is different from being God.

However, this is silly, since the Hebrews all thought of themselves as sons and daughters of God.

When Jesus said He was *"THE"*Son of God, the high priest called it blasphemy, because to be *"THE"*Son of God is to make Himself out to be God.

To explain this:

My father is a Speray. I'm a son of a Speray. Thus we are both one and the same family of Sperays.

Jesus never said He was the Father. Father and Son are two different Persons, but both are of the same Godhead. This is why Jesus says to Baptize in the Name (not names) of the Father, Son, and Holy Ghost.

The Hebrews understood this and had the Romans crucify Jesus for making the claim.

Jesus claims to be the way, the truth and the life. (John 14:6) Man can only find a way, know the truth, or have life, where as God can be the way, the truth, and the life.

Both God the Father and Jesus are called the Alpha and Omega in the Holy Bible. See (Rev. or Apoc. 1:8 and 22:12-13)

Now one may argue that if Jesus is God then the Holy Bible also contradicts itself.

For instance, we have the Holy Scriptures tell us that Jesus grew in knowledge and wisdom, that He says that the Father is greater than He, that He knows not the Day, or that he asks questions Himself to get information.

If Jesus is God, He would not need to grow in knowledge and wisdom, nor would He be less than the Father. He would know the Day and would not need to ask any questions since He would already know all the answers.

To answer this, we must realize what perspectives the Holy Scriptures are written in.

In all appearances, Jesus did grow in knowledge and wisdom but not actually.

Jesus is less than the Father from the standpoint of His nature. Human nature is less than the Divine Nature. From the standpoint of Christ's Divine Nature, He is equal to the Father.

The above could apply to the question of not knowing, but a better explanation is that Jesus does know the Day but says that He doesn't since it is not for men to know. This is known as equivocation.

Of course, this may appear to show that Jesus is a liar and the Holy Bible states that God cannot deceive nor be deceived.

There are different forms of deception and God cannot deceive man into sin nor could He be deceived into sin. But God can most certainly deceive as it is also written in (Second Thessalonians 2:11) that God will send a strong delusion. This act is one of permission by withholding grace.

It is argued that a lie is a lie plain and simple and it is always a sin. However, equivocation is a little different. It's expected on certain occasions.

A time of war as a spy is one example. To save a life without endangering others is another, and of course, the time when Christ does it. The Apostles know that Christ is using equivocation.

As for asking questions, Jesus does not need the information due to ignorance but for the purpose of having men own up.

When my son hides after doing something wrong, I may know where he is hiding but I will still ask where he is.

God does the same thing. We see the example of Adam and Eve hiding and God asks, *"Where are you?"*(Gen. 3:9) God knows but wants Adam to own up.

It may not always be for sin but merely to have man come forward.

We see Jesus asked who touched Him as He felt power go out from him. (Mark 5:31) Jesus knows who touched Him but wants us to come out from the shadows and not to be afraid.

The Holy Bible only appears to contradict itself. It doesn't actually do so.

ISLAM

Muslims from the religion of Islam do not believe Jesus died on the cross. However, their religion comes 600 years after the fact based on the testimony of one man claiming to hear it from an angel claiming to be of God.

Christians have already been forewarned of such an event.

St. Paul said, *"if we, or an angel from heaven, should preach to you a gospel contrary to that which we preached to you, let him be accursed. As we have said before, so now I say again, If any one is preaching to you a gospel contrary to that which you received, let him be accursed."*(Galatians 1:8-9)

Muslims should think long and hard about the foundation of their religion of which they stake their very souls. It is based solely from the testimony of one man and his visiting angel.

What reason is there to believe in Mohammed?

What reason does the angel give to believe he was from Heaven as opposed to hell?

The foundation is too weak especially compared to the foundation of Christianity.

Other non-Christians also hold that Jesus never actually died on the cross and the Apostles were only mistaken.

This argument doesn't hold up on three levels.

First, this is an insult to the Romans who were the experts in killing. They pierced his heart and knew Jesus had died. Of all the criminals they put to death, Jesus was the one man they were not going to fail in their duty in putting to death. See (John 19:34)

Secondly, the guard assigned to guard His tomb missed the stone being rolled back, told the chief priests what happened, and then took money from the priests to lie about it. See (Matthew 27:62-66 and Matthew 28:11-14)

Thirdly, those who first saw Jesus after He resurrected didn't recognize Him at first. (Luke 24:1-49 and John 14:11-18)

All the Apostles saw Jesus ascend into Heaven. (Luke 24:50 and Acts 1:6-11)

There was no mistake about it.

THE MIRACLES

Another reason to believe Jesus is God would be due to all the fantastic miracles that concern Christianity.

The documented raisings of the dead, not to be confused with near-death experiences, are a powerful testimony to the truth of Christianity.

The miracle of Lanciano, which is an on-going scientifically examined miracle, is a wonderful modern day miracle. It is over 1,300 years old.

In 1917, over 70,000 people including non-believers witnessed the miracle of the sun at Fatima, which was foretold months in advance to the very day. Two reporters for the local newspapers recorded the event as eyewitnesses. The surrounding area was soaked after a rainfall and yet was completely dry within the ten-minute miracle. Wet clothing was dry and looked pressed. All the people thought the world was coming to an end, and afterwards even non-believers believed.

The numerous incorrupt bodies of Catholic saints, especially those who were never embalmed but retain perfect body appearance with no mummification such as St. Catherine of Laboure who died in 1879, can be viewed in person to this very day.

Perhaps the greatest modern day miracle is the miracle of Hiroshima where eight Jesuits living eight blocks from the center of the atomic bomb blast of 1945 emerged alive and well.

Most everything within a mile-radius of the blast was annihilated, including the cathedral immediately next to the home of the eight priests. While many others survived, the priests were exposed.

Father Hubert Schiffer, a German-born missionary, described it as a blinding white light unlike anything he had ever seen before... and afterwards, there was only silence and it remained completely silent.

When Father Hubert was asked on American TV how they all survived the nuclear blast, he gave them the answer, *"In that house, we were living the message of Fatima."*

All these great miracles testify to the truth of Christianity.

MAJOR EXORCISMS

Finally, exorcisms also testify to the truth of Christianity.

Unfortunately, many exorcisms are due most likely to the cause of mental illness or performed hoaxes.

Those that are real are divided into two categories, minor and major.

Nearly all of them fall under the minor category. These are not to be confused with the type that comes with the sacrament of Baptism, which is a type of minor exorcism.

The minor exorcisms can be successfully performed by anyone in any religion though only through the name of Jesus. Although, it is not advised and under most circumstances forbidden for Catholics to perform such exorcisms since only priests are permitted.

Minor exorcisms are extremely strange occurrences but nothing that would convince a non-believer.

The major exorcisms are extraordinary events and can only be successfully performed by Catholic priests. Non-believers who are asked to help in major exorcisms have testified that horrifying or nasty images are projected into their minds along with telepathy.

Sins, known only to them, are exposed in detail by the possessed. Levitation and teleportation accompany such exorcisms. Knowledge of foreign languages never before studied by the one possessed is used in great detail. The ability to craw up walls or extrude large amounts of body fluids that would be impossible for a body to retain are things found in major exorcisms. Sometimes the possessed can get fixed into impossible body positions and even then men cannot undo them.

Such exorcisms can last for many years and sometimes priests suffer severe injury or death.

The exorcists themselves have testified to these and many more supernatural occurrences.

Neither madness nor trick explains these happenings and yet the exorcisms are successful.

I would call all these good reasons to believe Jesus is God.

Ultimately, it comes down to faith, but not without good reason.

If Jesus is God then to reject Him is to reject God. If Jesus were not God, then to accept Him would be accepting a false god.

The choice is up to us.

What reasons are there not to believe in Jesus? I see no logical ones.

If this is not the case for you, then do your objections outweigh the reasons just given?

Whatever the case may be it is illogical to say that it doesn't matter.

3. The Papacy in a Nutshell

The Catholic Papacy may be the most misunderstood doctrine in Christianity. Even some theologians misunderstand it and therefore misrepresent it.

The papacy is the office of the Catholic Faith, which constitutes the visible Head of Christianity, united to Christ the invisible Head of the Church. Because Christ ever remains the Head of the Church, this divine institution is never headless. The Catholic Church claims the Apostle Peter as being the first Roman Pontiff or pope and having with him successors.

The office must be distinguished from the man holding the office. The pope is addressed as Holy Father or Your Holiness, but these titles are not necessarily describing the pope himself, but the office.

In fact, the pope may not be holy at all. Although many have been saintly, it is true that many have also been wicked, even monstrous. I'm sure one of the agonies during the Passion of Our Lord Jesus was visualizing the future of His Church and the devils that would occupy the holy office He established for the good of civilization.

How many of those popes have *"spurned the Son of God, and profaned the blood of the covenant by which he was sanctified, and outraged the Spirit of grace,"* and ended up in hell? I'm sure many of the good popes didn't make it straight to heaven either. *"And unto whomsoever much is given, of him much shall be required."* (Luke 12:48)

There is an interesting story about the great Pope Innocent III who appeared on fire in purgatory to St. Lutgarde. The dead pope told the saint that he was supposed to go to hell for a mortal sin but was given the grace of final penitence at death.

The office of the Roman Pontiff is perpetually the head of Christianity, but that doesn't mean there will always be a pope holding the office. The office becomes vacant every time a pope dies, relinquishes the office, loses the faith, becomes schismatic, or becomes doubtful.

All of the above are possible, even if it's common to hear *"Catholic"* apologists argue to the contrary. Historically, there have been at least two popes, and perhaps a few more, who have relinquished the office and several have been doubtful. Never has one lost the faith or become schismatic, although this is a possibility.

Whenever the papacy becomes vacant, it is known as an interregnum period. *Sede vacant* means the Chair of Peter is vacant. The pope is ordinarily elected from the College of Cardinals that was constructed and formed from the previous popes. This arrangement has not always been the law. It fact, popes have been elected by the people, forced onto the throne by the emperor, and some were just acknowledged as popes without cause. The current law that cardinals are to elect future popes would not apply under extraordinary circumstances such as the possible extinction of the College of Cardinals.

Since the head of the household is the man (Ephesians 5, Numbers 1:4), the pope, which means *"papa"*, is the head of the household of God, the Church (Ephesians 2:19-22, I Timothy 3:15). Therefore, the first requirement for the papacy is to be a man. It should be noted that every bishop and priest is *"a"* pope but they are not *"the"* pope. This is why only men can be priests and bishops. Just as the terms king and prince denote men, so too, the very word priest denotes fatherhood.

Since there are laws for the election of the pope, the second requirement is a valid election that follows the necessary laws thereof.

The third requirement for a valid election is the formal consent of the elected.

Since the pope is the head or overseer of the Church and particularly Rome, he must also be a bishop, which means overseer. Therefore, the fourth requirement (only if needed) is to ordain the elected a priest and consecrate him bishop.

Lastly, the fifth requirement is to hold fast to Catholic teachings after one becomes a pope, or else he automatically loses the office. This doctrine comes from the universal teaching of all the popes and saints who have ever spoken on the issue and supported by canon law, not to mention pure logic. A man cannot be head of the Church, if he is not a member.

The pope is a man like all men; he is a sinful and fallible man. He does not have some special connection with God as if he can hear God directly. He does not necessarily know the Catholic Faith better than the rest of Christianity.

The pope is very limited in his authority. He cannot do or teach whatever he wants just because he holds the highest office in the Church. His duty is to guard the truth and teach and preach the Gospel. If necessary, he may expound on the Deposit of Faith by defining or proclaiming a doctrine as part of the Christian Faith.

He cannot invent some novel teaching and proclaim it as part of the Christian Faith. It must only come from the Deposit of Faith, which can be seen and understood in light of Holy Scripture and Sacred Tradition.

Sacred Tradition (not to be confused with traditions of men) is a combination of the teaching of Christ and the Apostles, not written down, along with the practice of the Church.

When the pope makes proclamations and definitions as the pope, he is infallible. Infallibility is a special chrism or gift of the pope. It means that the pope cannot err in teaching the faithful under very specific circumstances.

When the pope teaches *ex cathedra* (from the Chair) meaning as the head of the whole Church to the whole Church on anything regarding faith and morals to be held as a truth never to be altered, he is infallible. It is a preventive measure given to him by Christ and the Holy Ghost to prevent heresy (known as the *"Gates of Hell"* or *"Powers of Death"*) from ever being taught by the Church.

Just as God used fallible men to write the infallible Holy Scriptures, God now uses fallible men to teach the Gospel of the Holy Scriptures infallibly. The Bible needs some infallible interpretations having boundaries and limits on other interpretations, or else it's every man for himself. The Bible itself was not just assumed to be infallible. There is not some inspired table of contents and even if did, it wouldn't necessarily make it so. Many false writings claim divine inspiration.

The Canon of Scripture (books in the Bible) has been infallibly determined by the Church to be infallible. Of course, the Scriptures are infallible if they are God-breathed, but we would not know what precisely which of these God-breathed books are God-breathed without the affirmation of the Church. The Bible was determined and affirmed by Sacred Tradition and the final authority in the Church, the pope. Therefore, without an infallible Church and pope, the Bible itself would not be known, at least, not infallibly.

Besides guarding the Truth, and teaching and proclaiming the Gospel, and defining doctrine, the pope is a symbol of unity. Actually, his office is the symbol of unity since unity can be maintained without a pope. The teaching office, whether vacant or filled, along with all those things that have been previously taught by that office, hold the unity needed for the Church.

The papal office is a justifiable part of true Christianity. In the Gospel of Matthew 16:18-19, we see Christ saying that He will build His Church and then give the keys to the kingdom of heaven to Peter.

The argument whether Peter or Christ is the rock is a moot point. It doesn't really matter. Although historically, every Church father who said anything about this verse, said that it was either Peter and/or Peter's confession of Faith that is the Rock on which Christ built His Church. None said the Rock in this verse was meant to be understood as Christ.

Peter's name obviously means rock, stone, or small pebble, which most probably means that it was about Peter and his faith since this is the context, but again, it doesn't really matter. What matters are the keys to the kingdom.

Christ uses a future tense of the word that He will give Peter the keys sometime in the future. Although, Jesus gives all the Apostles the power to bind and loose in Matt. 18, this should not be confused with the special binding and loosing given specifically to Peter in Matt. 16 after Jesus says that He will give him the keys. This is understood in light of the rest of Holy Writ that speaks of Peter as head of the others.

For instance, Peter is mentioned throughout Holy Scripture as *"Peter and the others"* or some phrase such as this. He also is mentioned in the Holy Bible over one hundred and ninety times. The next closest Apostle most mentioned is John found under thirty times. Peter is clearly understood as one with special significance.

Also, if we turn to Isaiah 22:22, we see that Eli'akim is given the key to the kingdom of David even though Eli'akim is not the king. It is clear that Christ was drawing from this very passage. Jesus is the eternal Son and King and will place under Him one who will be given the keys to the eternal kingdom.

It might be argued that Eli'akim is given a key where as Peter is given keys, therefore, Christ was not drawing-out from the Isaiah passage. I would suggest that such an argument is looking into Holy Scripture anachronistically since the one making the argument is looking for a way out of having to see Peter as the only one holding the keys.

The passage in Isaiah also denotes that the key holder has successors to maintain the authority of keeping in or out of the house or kingdom. Since Jesus was clearly drawing from this image, the intention of Christ is that Peter would have successors with authority of keeping in or out (binding and loosing) of the Church.

One might argue that if the papacy is so important and constitutes what Catholics claim, we would see Christ actually giving Peter the keys in the Holy Bible. The problem with this argument is that the keys represent authority and succession. There is not an actual set of keys. There is no need to see the ceremony, if any, that Peter becomes the actual head of the Church. It is understood.

This brings us to the Council of Jerusalem.

Another argument against Peter's supreme authority is that James appears to be head of the Church at the Council of Jerusalem in the Book of Acts; Chapter 15. This argument most definitely is an anachronistic viewpoint, since there is no reason to believe it. Those who make this argument are the ones trying to look for a reason not to believe Peter is at the helm.

Again, Peter settles the matter after much debate in Acts 15:7.

Barnabas and Paul confirm the truth in verse 12 and then James puts in his two-cents worth.

James has to say, *"Listen to me"* since his words need everybody's attention unlike Peter's, who already has everybody's attention.

Peter does not have to say, *"listen to me"* because they listen and when he spoke, *"the assembly kept silence"*(Acts 15:12).

James then gives his judgment on how Peter's words are to be applied.

Again, it is Peter most mentioned in the Book of Acts.

"Peter stood up among the brethren...and said"(Acts 1:15).

"Peter standing with the eleven, lifted up his voice and addressed them"(Acts 2:14).

"Peter and the rest of the Apostles"(Acts 2:37). *"Peter said to them"*(Acts 2:38).

"Peter saw it and addressed the people"(Acts 3:12).

"Peter, filled with the Holy Spirit, said to them"(Acts 4:8).

"Peter and the apostles answered"(Acts 5:29).

Peter is mentioned another forty-nine times in the Book of Acts alone. There are other verses to show Peter is the shepherd over Christ's flock but these suffice.

One might ask, *"Where does the Bible say Peter was pope?"*

Pope is a term given the office years later. The office is what we are looking for, not the name of the office. The Church gave the office the name.

What we see in the Holy Bible is Peter as the head of the Apostles who alone is given the keys signifying that he has been given special authority and successors. Since the Church is likened as the *"household of God"* then *"pope"* is a very proper title.

Why does Peter describe himself as a fellow elder if he is the head elder? Peter is a fellow elder. Head elder doesn't mean that he is no longer a fellow elder. Also, Peter is simply being humble by not referring to himself as chief. Modern popes also use the phrase *"fellow elders"* in their letters, encyclicals, and exhortations.

Why do we see the Apostles' asking who is the greatest in the kingdom of heaven if Peter is understood to be the greatest? Peter's status in authority is not the same as his status in holiness. Popes may even go to hell. For all we know, John may have been holier than Peter.

The Holy Bible is only one avenue to see the papacy. The other is history.

Early Church fathers list Peter and his successors. No other Apostle has a list of successors. Only Peter, because the early Church understood that Peter's line of succession is the only one that really counts since it is his office that makes for the final authority among the elders or bishops of the Church.

As early as the end of the first century, Peter's successor Clement (mentioned in Philippians 4:3 according to historians) wrote letters to the Corinthians as head of the Church telling the Corinthians that they must be united to Rome. Yes, Clement uses the axiom we fellow elders at Rome, but it is understood that Clement is the chief elder as the letter is attributed to him.

Finally, the pope does not always call councils as the Emperor Constantine called Nicea.

The pope does not always use his authority as he ought. The pope does not know everything. His knowledge is limited. The pope can be mistaken when not speaking to the whole world as pope on faith and morals.

The pope can be resisted if he commands one to sin. The pope can unjustly excommunicate or anathematize. When he does such things, the faithful are duty bound to correct him.

However, the faithful must distinguish between the bad or unjust popes from the antipopes. Popes can be wicked and unjust but popes cannot be heretics or schismatics.

Antipopes are false claimants to the papacy and there have been many in church history. Only one pope can reign at a time. All claimants to the papacy when a true pope is already reigning are antipopes. Antipopes have no authority whatsoever. They are to be rejected.

The way one can determine whether one is a true pope or antipope is first to determine if the claimant holds the Catholic faith whole and inviolate. If he doesn't, then he is not pope. If his election created reasonable doubt, then by that fact alone, he is not pope.

The papacy is the logical extension to Christ founding His Church. As implied earlier, without the papacy, every man indeed would be for himself. There could never be a final say that would universally be accepted by the whole. There would never be any real doctrinal unity without the papacy.

The historic facts clearly prove that Peter has been recognized as the first pope with Linus, Cletus, and Clement as his immediate successors. Peter's line of successors has been recognized by virtually all who claim Christianity until the sixteenth century. There is no logical reason to disbelieve in the papacy as being part of true Christianity, unless, of course, one rejects as did the original Protestants, the two-thousand-year historic understanding of the Church and Christianity.

4. Objections to Purgatory Answered in a Nutshell

Imagine if a Christian, or anybody for that fact, rejected the existence of Heaven or Hell. Would such a person be considered a Christian? Of course not, since Christians must hold to all articles of Faith, such as the existence of Heaven or Hell.

Yet, Purgatory is also an article of Faith. It is as real and true as Heaven and Hell. All those who claim to be Christian but knowingly reject Purgatory are heretics. Heretics are non-Christians who claim to be Christian.

Purgatory is the place and state of existence, which the justified man is purified before witnessing the Beatific Vision. This purification could be for the atonement or punishment of forgiven mortal or venial sins, and for the inordinate love of self, others, or the world.

Purgatory comes from the word meaning, to purge.

There are 4 main objections heretics use for rejecting Purgatory.

Objection number 1: Purgatory is not found in the Holy Bible; therefore it is not an article of Faith.

There are many words not found in the Holy Bible that must be believed such as Holy Trinity, hypostatic union, Incarnation, or even *"bible."* These things are based on a deduction of the facts using sound logic and reason. The Canon of Holy Scripture (Books of the Holy Bible) are not even found implicitly in the Holy Bible, but must be believed based on an authority outside of Scripture.

All of Scripture is most certainly inspired and can be used for teaching, defending, and promoting the Faith, but never does the Scripture say that it ALONE constitutes everything that must be believed. If it did, then you could not even follow it, since it does not give an inspired table of contents. How ironic heretics would use such an illogical argument. This is a tradition of man that nullifies the Word of God.

Be that as it may, Purgatory is most certainly found in the Holy Bible by way of implication, just as the Holy Trinity and Incarnation.

(Apocalypse or Rev. 21:27) says nothing unclean can enter Heaven. This implies that all men must be made clean before entering Heaven.

(First Corinthians 3:9-17) states: *"For we are God's fellow workers; you are God's field, God's building. According to the grace of God given to me, like a skilled master builder I laid a foundation, and another man is building upon it. Let each man take care how he builds upon it. For no other foundation can any one lay than that which is laid, which is Jesus Christ. Now if any one builds on the foundation with gold, silver, precious stones, wood, hay, straw – each man's work will become manifest; for the Day will disclose it, because it will be revealed with fire; and the fire will test what sort of work each one has done. If the work which any man has built on the foundation survives, he will be saved, but only as through fire. Do you not know that you are God's temple and that god's Spirit dwells in you? If any one destroys God's temple, God will destroy him. For God's temple is holy, and that temple you are."*

The Day is Judgment Day. The temple is man. Gold, silver, and precious stones represents good works. Wood, hay, and straw represent venial sins. Destruction of the temple is mortal sin.

Mortal sins are sins unto death, and venial sins are sins not unto death (First John 5:16-17). For instance, in (Matthew 5:19), Jesus states that they're certain sins men can commit, and even teach others to commit that sin, and they would be called least in the Kingdom of Heaven. Other sins however, Jesus says would cause men liable to hell fire. Therefore, different types of sins have different types of punishment.

"The person will be saved as going through the fire. Those who destroy the temple will themselves be destroyed." These verses are not about rewards because St. Paul was not only talking about rewards, but a JUDGMENT, and as been shown, this judgment varies.

Those who build with gold, silver, and precious stones will be rewarded (this is Heaven), those who build with wood, hay, and straw will suffer but will be saved as going through the fire (this is purgatory), and those who will not build but destroy the temple will themselves be destroyed (this is hell).

The Old Testament Book (Second Maccabees 12: 43-45) states: *"In doing this he acted in a very excellent and noble way, inasmuch as he had the resurrection of the dead in view; for if he were not expecting the dead to rise again, it would have been useless and foolish to pray for them in death. But if he did this with a view to the splendid reward that awaits those who had gone to rest in godliness, it was a holy and pious thought. Thus he made atonement for the dead that they might be freed from this sin"*

Why pray for those eternally lost in Hell or saved in Heaven? This Bible verse clearly references another place for those expiating sin. Because the doctrine of Purgatory so clear in this book of the Holy Bible, heretics eliminated it, precisely because this verse didn't square up with their systematic theology that rejects Purgatory.

Purgatory is Scriptural and it is logical. Its rejection is anti-scriptural and illogical.

Objection number 2: Purgatory is contrary to (First John 1:7) that a Christian is only purified by the blood of Jesus. Christ did it all and nothing can be added to His shedding of blood. Christ's atonement replaces any atonement needed by man. In other words, Christ's atonement on the Cross was not good enough if Purgatory is true.

The fact is (I John 1:7) says, *"The blood of Jesus purifies us from all sin."* not that *"we are purified only by the blood of Jesus."* However, Christ alone purifies and if it is not done on earth then it will be done later. Mortal sin takes one to hell, not Purgatory. Again, Purgatory is for the saved sinner who is purged of all imperfections, including the atonement of forgiven mortal and venial sins before entering Heaven, since nothing unclean can enter Heaven (Apoc. or Rev. 21:27).

The shedding of Christ's blood is applied to man through justification and sanctification. Christ's atonement is sufficient and complete. However, it must be applied and we must cooperate by doing our part designated to us by God.

Objection number 3: Purgatory does not fit into the theology that claims Christ's righteousness is only imputed to man's soul thereby justifying the man. This justification happens only once. (Rom. 4:8 and II Cor. 5:19) denote that sins no longer count against the justified and (Hebrew 10:14) says Christ has perfected for all time those who are sanctified.

The fact is Christ's righteousness is infused into man's soul, which actually makes the soul righteous. Imputation denotes a covering only. If it were merely imputed then the soul itself would remain unclean. Nothing unclean can enter Heaven; therefore an unclean man with a mere covering or imputation of righteousness would violate the very Word of God. Christ's righteousness must be infused or else no one could enter Heaven.

It does not happen only once. Justification is a process as Holy Scripture shows. Abraham *"believed God and it was reckoned to him as righteousness"* (Rom. 4:18-22). Paul was referring to (Gen. 15:6) where Abraham was given the promise of many descendants. This clearly shows Abraham was justified at the time he believed the promise.

"By faith Abraham obeyed...went out, not knowing where he was to go"(Heb. 11:8). This passage refers to (Gen. 12:1-4). We see clearly from Scripture that Abraham had saving Faith years before the promise in (Gen. 15). Abraham could not have saving faith if he were not already justified.

"Was not Abraham our father JUSTIFIED by works, when he offered his son Isaac upon the altar? It was reckoned to him as righteousness" (James 2:21-23). Abraham offered Isaac upon the altar in (Gen. 22) years after (Gen.15).

We have three instances where Abraham was re-justified by faith and works, denoting justification as a process.

It is true that St. Paul in Romans and Second Corinthians denotes that sins no longer count against the justified but this applies to past sins only, not future sins. St. Paul gives future senses of justification. *"We wait for the hope of justification"*(Gal. 5:5). He also states in (Heb 11:1) that faith is the assurance of things hoped for, the conviction of things not seen. If we know absolutely we are going to Heaven, where is our hope? Hope would not be hope if the object could be seen.

As for (Hebrews 10:14), St. Paul is referring that once sanctified than you a perfected forever provide that one does not sin again. Another translation is, *"Being made perfect forever those who are being sanctified."* 'Being' is a present participle that denotes an ongoing process.

Since justification and sanctification is a process. It can be said that Purgatory is the finishing process of sanctification. *"For our God is a consuming fire"*(Heb. 12:29).

God is constantly purifying us as we live on earth and it will continue after death if necessary. It is Christ who is doing the purifying by His justice. Purgatory is the application of Christ's atonement to our souls after death. Christ's atonement was perfect and complete, but it must be applied.

This objection arose with the ex-Catholics in the 16th century to create a new religion with a new theology. It is truly anti-Christian.

Objection number 4: Purgatory is contrary to the belief that Christ paid the complete sin debt meaning that He accomplished all that is needed without any cooperation from man.

Jesus tells Christians in (Matt. 6:12-15) in the Lord's Prayer to *"forgive us our debts as we forgive our debtors...If you forgive others their transgressions, your heavenly Father will forgive you. But if you do not forgive others, neither will your Father forgive your transgressions."*

If Jesus paid completely the sin debt of Christians, why would we need to ask the Father to forgive our debts if Jesus already paid them? Jesus even qualifies his next statement with an 'IF.' *"IF you do not forgive others, neither will your Father forgive your transgressions."* Why would the Father exact the same debt that Jesus supposedly just paid? Would God exact an unfair double payment? Of course not, therefore this objection is ridiculous and even blasphemous.

You will not find a Scripture passage state or imply that Christ paid the complete sin debt of man.

What Christ did on the Cross was redeem man by freeing him (saving) from absolute death. All men would absolutely go to hell without the Cross, but not necessarily granted Heaven (saved as in final salvation) or else all men would go to Heaven. Christ died for all men but He didn't grant all men salvation into Heaven.

God will save the man who cooperates with His grace by working, praying, and obeying. This is how man builds up the temple St. Paul was referring to in First Corinthians.

Provided man does not destroy the temple by mortal sin, his working, praying, and obeying will be tested. As gold is purified by fire, so too, man will be purified by the fire of God's justice. If a man's working, praying, and obeying are not perfect (wood, hay, and straw), that man will suffer loss but will be saved. This is Purgatory.

Purgatory can be bypassed altogether provided that man suffers all that is needed while on earth.

Interestingly, the proper understanding of Purgatory and salvation gives a new meaning to suffering on earth. All suffering becomes worthy of some cause especially when offered up in unity with the Cross of Christ.

Like fire on earth, suffering on earth can be useful and praiseworthy leading to a greater love for Our Lord, or it can be detrimental leading to rage, envy, and despair.

The suffering in Purgatory is a fire good only for purification.

Lastly, Purgatory is part of the historic Christian Faith. It is part of the Holy Gospel first delivered to the Apostles.

Christian worship was done in the early Church for the poor souls in Purgatory, as masses for the dead were commonplace, especially in the catacombs.

The historic practices come from this interpretation of these Scripture verses. Any other interpretation that would deny the existence of Purgatory would be contrary to history and logic.

The Holy Scriptures themselves tell us to hold fast to everything that has been taught and delivered from the beginning.

(II Thessalonians 2:15, Jude 1) Novel interpretations that run contrary to the historical teachings and practices are warned against by St. Paul in (II Timothy 4:3-4) and (Galatians 1:7-9.)

The rejection of Purgatory equals a gospel contrary to Christ.

5. What's Missing on Christmas in a Nutshell

Year after year, we see many people scrambling to buy gifts as the hustle and bustle of Christmas takes place. As each year passes, so-called Christians talk about how Christ is once again taken out of Christmas. As secularism creeps in, we are reminded over and over to remember the real reason for the season.

For many so-called Christians, the highlight of the season is the gathering of family and friends, eating, singing carols and going to church to praise God and calling to mind the birth of our Savior Jesus Christ.

On Christmas day in nearly every church service across America, indeed the world, the most important part of the service will be missing.

It will not be that Christ is forgotten, or taken out of Christmas, for it is in His Holy Name that these so-called Christians namely Evangelicals, Protestants, and Fundamentalists, and even neo-Catholics will come together. Rather, it is the Holy Mass that will be missing from Christmas. Hence the name 'Christ Mass' or the 'Mass of Christ'.

The Holy Mass is the supreme act of Christian worship. It is infinitely greater than any other form of Christian worship. It is the very life, death and Resurrection of Jesus being presented in a liturgical form so that the faithful can participate in Christ's own prayers and offering His sacrifice to the Father. It is called the Mass (Missa in Latin), because this liturgy concludes with the sending forth (missio) of the faithful.

The Mass was the code name for the worship service of the ancient Christians to keep pagan Rome from finding out and keep the heart of Christianity a secret.

At Holy Mass, not only is there prayer, singing, praising and hearing the Word of God, but also, Christ's supreme once-and-for-all sacrifice on the cross (Heb. 10:10), and His Resurrection is made present throughout time for all generations to enjoy the benefits of what Christ did and is doing for our sins.

The Mass is not a re-sacrifice, but the same sacrifice represented in an unbloody manner. Above all else, the Mass is the earthly participation in that sacrificial offering going on in Heaven where Jesus prays, and offers Himself up to the Father on our behalf.

Since the mission of Christ began at His birth, the worship service celebrating that day came to be known as Christ Mass or simply Christmas. We see this reality in Scripture with the practice of all faithful Christians throughout history.

In (Hebrews 9:23), the sacrifice of the Mass is explained: *"Therefore, it was necessary for the copies of the heavenly things to be purified by these rites, but the heavenly things themselves by better sacrifices than these."* Notice the plural sacrifices as a copy of the heavenly things.

(Hebrews 13:10) mentions, *"We have an altar."* An altar without a sacrifice would be meaningless.

We also see the Mass explained in the (First Letter to the Corinthians 11:17-34) clarifying the true nature of the Lord's Supper which clearly shows that it is not a mere symbol as the Evangelicals, Protestants, and Fundamentalists would have us to believe. Although, without a valid priesthood, they all can only have merely a symbolic Lord's Supper.

Speaking of the Lord, (Psalm 110) reads, *"Like Melchizedek, you shall be a priest forever."* As Melchizedek offered bread and wine, so too, Christ would offer up His body and blood in the form of bread and wine (Matt. 26:26-29.)

Christ commands us to do likewise (Luke 22:19.) This new sacrifice would be offered as Holy Writ has it, *"For from the Rising of the sun, even to its setting, my name is great among the nations; And everywhere they bring sacrifice to my name, and a pure offering."*(Malachi 1:11)

Only the Holy Mass can, and does fulfill this final prophecy of the Old Testament.

The Holy Mass (Lord's Supper) is a memorial, but not merely as a psychological remembrance as in non-Catholic services. It is a supernatural copy on Earth of the Heavenly things, viz, Christ continually offering His sacrifice to the Father as He sits at His right hand. Christians are invited to this sacrifice to receive Christ mysteriously on earth by literally eating His Flesh and drinking His Blood as we read in (Matt. 26:26-28, Mark 14:22-24. Luke 22:14-21, John 6:53-57, and I Cor. 11:23-26).

As many of the disciples thought it was a hard saying, (John 6:60) so too, did the Protestant Reformers of the 16th and continual centuries. The difference between the Jews of that time and the Reformers was the Jews recognized that Christ was not speaking symbolically.

To symbolically eat flesh and drink blood, meant to revile and hate the enemy by the ancient Jews, thereby rendering Christ's words ridiculous and silly since one would have to revile and hate Christ to have eternal life. Had Christ only meant it figuratively, the Jews would have not left Him. They knew well enough that Christ meant literally that His Flesh was real food and His Blood was real drink (John 6:56). Incidentally, it was here that Judas Iscariot left and stopped believing in Jesus (John 6:71).

Christ had warned them not to think of it as cannibalism for the flesh is no avail, but the spirit that gives life (John 6:63). In other words, it is a matter of faith, and will not happen in the bloody way that you are thinking. It is not only the Flesh but also the Soul and Divinity, and this is what gives life.

Christ had told them in (John 6:53-54), *"unless you eat the Flesh of the Son of Man and drink His Blood, you do not have life in you. Whoever eats my flesh and drinks my blood has eternal life, and I will raise him on the last day."*

The Reformers, however, didn't want to leave Christ as those particular Jews before them. So they changed the theology and created a whole new interpretation of Scripture to fit their understanding of salvation even though it would contradict 1500 years of Christian belief and practice.

Once the Real Presence of Jesus in the Holy Mass was denied, the Holy Mass ceased with those who separated with the true Church. Only the Traditional Roman Catholic and Eastern Orthodox Churches continue to have Jesus Christ substantially present while all the rest of Christianity (if you call them that) can only have Jesus in spirit, though, I would say not even in spirit would Christ be present if His Holy Mass was denied.

If we take another look at the story of Christmas, we see that Jesus was born in a town called Bethlehem, which means House of Bread. (Matt 2:1) Mary had laid Him in a manger, which is a feeding tough for animals. (Luke 2:7) Jesus says that He is the Bread that comes down from Heaven. (John 6:58) Who is the Lamb of God who is to be eaten (John 1:29, Matt. 26:26-28, Exodus 12:3-4, 8-9, 11, 14-16.)

These three prophetic readings in Holy Scripture shows what Christmas is really all about, viz, that Christ came into the world, for the purpose of dying, giving Himself to us in a mystery, and redeeming mankind by saving us from absolute death.

Christ and the Mass are a reality joined together. To deny the Mass would be to deny the mystery of Christ's salvific work for mankind.

When those Jews left, Jesus then asks, *"Will you also go away?"*(John 6:67) The Lord's question is answered by Peter, *"You have the words of eternal life."*

To receive in faith the gift of Christ's Body and Blood at Mass is to fulfill what Jesus intended for those who truly love and follow Him.

Taking the Mass out of Christmas is a rejection of the real reason for the season, which is ultimately that we remember Christ's birth as we receive Him in Holy Communion at the Holy Sacrifice of the Mass and be reminded, and prepared for His coming again in glory.

6. Catholic Confession in a Nutshell

Catholic Confession is a major stumbling block for many who might easily become Catholic if it were not for certain beliefs as this one.

However, for the Catholic, the sacrament of Confession or Reconciliation is so crucial that refusing to practice it is the same as refusing to be Christian. Rejecting Confession is ultimately rejecting Christ who instituted it. That's right; it was Jesus who gave us this sacrament. It is clearly mentioned in the Holy Bible when interpreted in the logical and historical context.

An accusation I occasionally hear from the common heretic is: Catholics have it so easy, they can go all week drinking, cursing, and smoking, etc, and go to a priest for confession on Saturday believing they are forgiven and turn around and do it all over again.

Yet, the very same heretic is the one who will go all week drinking, cursing and carrying on and then claims to go inside a room and confess secretly to God well aware that he will also do it all over again.

Question: Which would be harder: Going to a priest or secretly to God? Catholics are not looking for the easy way out, but rather, taking the route given to us by Christ.

The fact is good Catholics do not believe they can go on sinning with the presumption of having it all forgiven in Confession. It would be a sacrilege to abuse the Sacrament of Confession with sins one is not truly sorry for. Catholics must be truly repentant with the intention never to sin again. Without both of these elements, Confession is worthless and becomes a sin in itself.

However, is it so that those who claim to go to God in secret actually confess each and every individual sin? Do they actually confess each sin knowing God already knows each and every one of them? I'll let them answer that one.

Confessing each individual sin is an acknowledgment of what one actually did to offend Almighty God. It is much more profound than merely saying to God that you are sorry for your sins.

In trying to trap the Catholic, the common heretic will ask: Why do Catholics confess their sins to man instead of God since it would be blasphemy to believe man does what only God can do?

This is precisely what the Scribes and Pharisees did with Jesus several times. They accused him of doing only what God can do; and how did Christ answer them each time?

WHAT THE HOLY BIBLE SAYS

"And behold they brought to him a paralytic, lying on the bed; and when Jesus saw their faith he said to the paralytic, "Take heart, my son; your sins are forgiven." And behold, some of the scribes said to themselves, "This man is blaspheming." But Jesus, knowing their thoughts, said, "Why do you think evil in your hearts? For which is easier, to say, 'Your sins are forgiven,' or to say, 'Rise and walk'? But that you may know that the Son of man has authority on earth to forgive sins" –he then said to the paralytic "Rise, take up your bed and go home," And he rose and went home. When the crowds saw it, they were afraid, and they glorified God, who had given such authority to men." (Matthew 9:2-8)

Jesus did not tell them that he was God. He was acting and speaking in His Human Nature proving that He healed the soul of the paralytic by making him physically well. The last verse (8) says that men have been given this power, not so much as the miracle of the physical healing but rather the healing of the soul which the miracle proved had happened. It indicates that Jesus who came to forgive sins has also passed this on to his Church.

To better clarify Christ passing on His Divine power of forgiving sins to his Church we turn to other passages in Holy Writ:

"Jesus said to them again, "Peace be with you. As the Father has sent me, even so I send you. "And when he had said this, he breathed on them, and said to them, "Receive the Holy Spirit. If you forgive the sins of any, they are forgiven; if you retain the sins of any, they are retained."(John 20:21-23)

All the power given to Jesus by the Father, Christ now gives to his Apostles, not to any one else but only to his Apostles. Christ the God-man breathes the Spirit into his Apostles (just as God breathed life into Adam in Genesis) and gives them power of not only forgiving sins, but also the power of retaining them.

The Apostles could not forgive or retain sins unless someone confesses specific committed sins. There it is! The practice of confessing sins to man is found and justified in the Holy Bible Also, it has been practiced from the time of the Apostles Catholicism is the religion of the Holy Bible and Christian history.

Today, the common heretic continues to accuse Catholics of doing what they claim only God can do just as the Scribes and Pharisees did with Jesus. See other passages of Scripture such as in (John 8:3-11) when Jesus told the woman caught in Adultery *"Neither do I condemn you; go, and do not sin again."*

Or, in (Luke 7:36-50) when He told the woman who washed his feet, *"Your sins are forgiven."*

Yes, Jesus is God and can forgive sins, and just as He has the power to forgive sins we see Him passing it on to His Apostles in (John 20.)

Since these same Apostles were given the special power of forgiving sins so too they passed it on as it was passed on to them.

"All this is from God, who through Christ reconciled us to himself and gave us the ministry of reconciliation; that is, God was in Christ reconciling the world to himself, not counting their trespassed against them, and entrusting to us the message of reconciliation. So we are ambassadors for Christ, God making his appeal through us. "(II Corinthians 5:18-20)

The ministry of Reconciliation is the ministry of the Catholic priesthood. It was given only to those whom the power itself has been given. Ordinary layman can forgive sins committed against themselves but not on behalf of God as priests.

"Is any one among you sick? Let him call for the elders of the church, and let them pray over him, anointing him with oil in the name of the Lord; and the prayer of faith will save the sick man, and the Lord will raise him up; and if he ahs committed sins, he will be forgiven. Therefore confess your sins to one another, and pray for one another, that you may be healed. "(James 5:2-16)

Notice that it is the elders who have the power. Elders are the bishops and priests and no one appoints themselves bishops and priests. They must be ordained by bishops, who can trace that lineage of power from Christ.

For no one gives themselves the power to forgive and anoint, but must be received by someone who has been given this power by someone who has been given this power going back to the Apostles themselves. This is what Apostolic Succession is and it is the only way one receives the power to forgive sins, which ultimately comes from Jesus Christ himself.

For those who would like to argue these Scripture verses and give a different spin on them, I would like to add that by doing so would be contrary to the historical interpretation and practice.

For Catholics, Confession is practiced because it has always been the practice of Apostolic Times, which the Scriptures and history indicate. For the common heretics who try to base their religion on what they think the Bible is saying to them is actually anti-Scriptural and anti-historical because the Scriptures themselves tell us to hold to everything that has been taught and delivered from the beginning. (II Thessalonians 2:15, Jude 1) Novel interpretations that run contrary to the historical teachings and practices are warned against by St. Paul in (II Timothy 4:3-4) and (Galatians 1:7-9.)

Rejecting Catholic Confession equals a gospel contrary to Christ.

7. The Truth about the Blessed Virgin Mary in a Nutshell

The good Catholic puts Jesus Christ at the center of his life. As for the Blessed Virgin Mary, he loves and honors her as the highest of all of God's creation, as Catholics believe God Himself holds her.
She is not worshiped in adoration but in honor only.

Worship can mean adoration (latria) or mere honor (dulia or hyperdulia). Catholics do not honor her any more than the great honor already bestowed on her by God by making her His own mother. Just as Christ obeyed the Law of honoring His mother and Father, so we imitate Christ.

Catholics most certainly pray to her as they do all the angels and saints.

Although all worship (adoration) is prayer, not all prayer is worship. The primary definition of pray is *"to ask, implore, and beseech."* Praying is the only form of communication we have with Heaven. When prayer is attributing divinity, it must be directed to God alone.

To pray to the dead is condemned by God, but those in Heaven are not dead. Catholics pray to Mary and the saints as a form of communication, because they're alive in Christ.

Catholics believe Christ is the one mediator between God and man and that salvation comes only from Him and through Him.

Catholics do not believe that God is too big for us to go straight to Him, because we go straight to Him every day. However, we do ask those older brothers and sisters and mother who have entered Heaven to pray for us and to help us in need, because they are instruments of God's grace.

Is this unbiblical? Not at all! They are the cloud of witnesses who are concerned with our salvation. (Hebrews 12:1) Mary and the saints are not dead but alive in Christ. We are in the love of Christ as those who have gone before us. Not even death can separate us from the love of Christ (Romans 8:38) and we who belong to Christ belong to His Body the Church. We cannot say we don't need others in the Body of Christ (I Cor. 12:18-20, 24-25) especially the saints.

The Holy Bible says the prayer of a righteous man avails much. (James 5:16)

Who are more righteous than the saints in Heaven? After all we petition Christians on earth to pray for us (I Timothy 2:1-3), and this doesn't run contrary to the doctrine that Christ is the one mediator. It is through Christ we pray for one another.

Why not petition those who have gone before us glorified in the Body of Christ who are concerned with our salvation?

This is what praying to Mary and saints is all about. Our Father in Heaven wants us to have a relationship with Mary and our older brothers and sisters in Heaven since after all; we are one big family who will one day be together for all eternity.

We call Mary the *"EVER"* Virgin because she did not have other children. The brethren of the Lord are not her children. The New Testament mentions *"brothers"* and *"sisters"* of the Lord in (Matt. 12:46; Matt. 13:55; Mark 3:31–34; Mark 6:3; Luke 8:19–20; John 2:12, 7:3, 5, 10; Acts 1:14; 1 Cor. 9:5).

"Brother" (Greek: adelphos or plural Adelphoi) and *"sister"* (adelphe) do not always mean full or half blood brother and sister.

The Old Testament shows that *"brother"* could mean any male relative from whom you are not descended. Male relatives from whom you are descended are known as *"fathers"* and all generations who are descended from you are your "sons" as well as cousins, those by marriage, or by law.

Lot is called Abraham's *"brother"*(Gen. 14:14), even though being the son of Haran, Abraham's brother (Gen. 11:26–28), he was actually Abraham's nephew.

Jacob is called the *"brother"*of his uncle Laban (Gen. 29:15). Kish and Eleazar were the sons of Mahli. Kish had sons of his own, but Eleazar had no sons, only daughters, who married their *"brethren,"* the sons of Kish. These *"brethren"* were really their cousins (1 Chr. 23:21–22).

(Deut. 23:7; Neh. 5:7; Jer. 34:9) refers to kinsman. See also the reference to the forty-two *"brethren"*of King Azariah (2 Kgs. 10:13–14) and (2 Sam. 1:26; Amos 1:9) refers to friends.

Be that as it may, there was no word for cousin in Hebrew or Aramaic and the word brother was used to identify them. The Greek word for cousin is anepsios but the New Testament writers translated by transliterating the Hebrew and Aramaic idiom into the Greek text.

We also see this in the Septuagint. The Septuagint was a Greek version of the Hebrew Bible, which came from the Hellenistic Jews 100 years BC. It was this version of the Bible that Christ used as the quotations found in the New Testament came from the Septuagint.

The English translators continued to use the same Hebrew word to identify all kinsmen. A close look at the text will clue us in on which kinsmen the word brother(s) might be or cannot be.

When Mary was told by the Angel Gabriel that she would conceive a son, she asked, *"How shall this happen, since I do not know man?"*(Luke 1:34)

The early Church Fathers interpreted this (and rightly so) to mean that Mary had made a vow of virginity even through married life. Why ask the question if this were not the case? After all, if Mary planned on having children with Joseph she would not have asked the question. Her marriage with Joseph was the rare type of living like brother and sister.

The first heretic to come up with the idea that Mary had other children was Helvidius in 380 AD. St Jerome in his treatise *"On the Perpetual Virginity of the Blessed Mary"* used Holy Scripture and the writings of earlier Fathers as St. Ignatius of Antioch, St. Polycarp (disciple of St John the Apostle), and Justin Martyr to completely debunk Helvidius' position which Jerome called *"novel, wicked, and daring affront to the faith of the whole world."*

The following is somewhat how St Jerome argued.

The finding of Jesus in the Temple at age twelve did not hint of the idea that Mary had other children. (Luke 2:41–51). Jesus was known as *"the son of Mary"*(Mark 6:3), not as *"a son of Mary."* Never do we see other children in the Gospels being referred to as children of Mary.

At the foot of the Cross, Jesus entrusted his mother to John (John 19:26-27). John's blood mother Salome was also at the foot of the Cross and if Jesus had other full blood brothers, why make Mary a mother to John who already has a mother? What about Mary's other sons?

The answer is that Mary never had any other child. Heretics argue *that "brethren of the Lord"*must be interpreted as full blood brothers because of other Scripture verses.

(Matthew 1:25): *"And he did not know her till she brought forth her firstborn son."*

Heretics fail to understand that *"till"* here does not always mean until something else happens. We see this word several times in Holy Writ. In (II Sam. 6:23), *"Michal the daughter of Saul had no children till the day of her death."* Does this mean that she had children after her death? Of course not.

In (Deuteronomy 34:6), speaking about Moses, *"and no man hath known of his sepulcher until this present day."* Does this mean that they know now? Of course not.

In (Genesis 8:6-7) speaking about Noah, *"after that forty days were passed Noe, opening the window of the ark which he had made, sent forth a raven: Which went forth and did not return till the waters were dried up upon the earth."* Does this mean the raven returned? Of course not.

Just as till or until does not work to mean some future event in these verses, it also does not imply in (Matthew 1) to mean that Mary and Joseph had relations after the birth of Christ.

First-born also doesn't imply that there is a second or third-born. As we see in (Exodus 12:2; Numbers 3:12) the Hebrews understood the meaning of first-born to be the child that opens the womb. The first-born son was to be sanctified under the Law. (Exodus 34:20) That child will always be thought of as the first-born regardless.

As for the brothers of the Lord who are mentioned, we know that the mother of James (the Less or Younger) was also named Mary.

When we cross reference the Gospels on the women standing beneath the cross we get a clear picture who is who: *"among whom were Mary Magdalene and Mary the mother of James and Joseph, and the mother of the sons of Zebedee"* (Matt. 27:56)

57

"There were also women looking on from afar, among whom were Mary Magdalene, and Mary the mother of James the younger and of Joses, and Salome"(Mark 15:40).

"But standing by the cross of Jesus were his mother, and his mother's sister, Mary the wife of Clopas, and Mary Magdalene" (John 19:25).

We see that Salome is the mother of the sons of Zebedee (James the Greater and John) and the mother of James and Joseph is the wife of Clopas.

Elsewhere (Matt. 10:3) we see that James is also the son of Alphaeus. This Alphaeus is the same person as Clopas. The Aramaic name for Alphaeus can be rendered in Greek either as Alphaeus or as Clopas.

Some have argued that Alphaeus took a Greek name similar to his Jewish name, the way Saul took the name Paul. James the Less or Younger (brother of the Lord) is the son of Mary and Clopas (Alphaeus). The other *"brethren"* are the actual full blood brothers of James, which means they are not the sons of the Virgin Mary.

There are other arguments to demonstrate Mary's perpetual virginity, but the above arguments alone suffice.

The doctrine of the Immaculate Conception means that Mary was conceived in her mother Anne's womb without the stain of original sin. Original sin is the deprivation of sanctifying grace with the stain of a corrupt nature.

Mary was preserved from this sin by God's grace from the first instant of her existence. She was born and remained throughout her whole life immaculate. Never did she sin nor was affected with a corrupt nature.

This doesn't mean she is almighty, all knowing, or equal to God. The Angels in Heaven have not sinned and we don't think of them as being equal to God.

It means that she has completed what Eve failed in the beginning. It means she is the perfect model for the Church. If the imperfect St. Paul said to imitate him as a model (I Cor. 4:13, 11:1, Philippians 3:17), how much more than the perfect Virgin Mary?

The Immaculate Conception of the Blessed Virgin Mary is most certainly justified from the Holy Bible.

First, (Genesis 3:15) can be used to identify Mary, who is at enmity with Satan. This comes right after the Original Sin of Adam and Eve.

Here, Holy Scripture says there will be a woman and whose seed will both be at enmity with Satan. The historical Christian faith has always identified Jesus as the *"New Adam"* but also Mary as the *"New Eve."* Incidentally, Jesus identified his mother as *"woman"* at the wedding feast at Cana (John 2:4) and again at the foot of the cross (John 25:26). Was Jesus reminding us of the prophecy of Genesis 3:15?

Secondly, the Angel Gabriel's greeting to Mary demonstrates her purity and perfection. The angel Gabriel said, *"Hail, full of grace, the Lord is with you"* (Luke 1:28). *"Full of grace"* is a translation of the Greek word kecharitomene. It therefore expresses a characteristic quality of Mary as it is a title.

The traditional translation, *"full of grace, "* is by far the best translation for it best captures what the Angel is conveying, rather than the poor translation *"highly favored daughter. "*

No doubt, Mary is the highly favored daughter of God, but the Greek implies much more. Also, it never mentions the word for daughter.

Kecharitomene is a perfect passive participle of charitoo, meaning *"to fill or endow with grace."* Since this term is in the perfect tense, it indicates that Mary was graced from the beginning up until the present.

Mary was always full of God's grace and she enjoyed that position throughout her whole life. She is the Immaculate Conception.   Period!

The doctrine of the Immaculate Conception was officially defined by Pope Pius IX in 1854. Heretics claim the doctrine was an invention of the Church at that time.

Doctrines are defined formally when controversy arises that needs to be settled or when the Church believes such definitions will draw men closer to God.

Many doctrines and beliefs took years for the Church to define. The Holy Trinity was defined in 325 AD and the Holy Bible was first defined in 380 AD. These were not inventions of the Church but definitions and declarations to clarify the Christian Faith.

Heretics say that Mary was a sinner because of (Rom. 3:23) *"all have sinned"* and because Mary said her *"spirit rejoices in God my Savior"* (Luke 1:47), and only a sinner needs a Savior.

It is true that Mary needed a Savior. However, unlike the rest of mankind, Christ saved her from absolute death by prevention. Mary is perfect because Christ saved her in anticipation at the moment of her conception.

Just as a drowning man is saved by being pulled out of the deep waters, Mary was prevented from falling in and even getting wet. Just as a man in a deep pit is saved by being pulled out, Mary is prevented from falling into the pit in the first place and being stained with the mud below.

She has more reason to call God her Savior than we do, because he saved her in an even more glorious manner!

As for (Romans 3:23), *"all have sinned",* we know that infants have not nor could not sin, and even St. Paul in (Romans 9:11) implies such when referring to Jacob and Esau.

The extreme mentally ill cannot sin since they have not the ability to reason.

Jesus never sinned (Heb. 4:15).

Both Mary and Jesus followed the Law of Moses of making sin offerings but this was to identify themselves with sinners, not indicate they were sinners needing to make an offering for some sin.

Since there are clear exceptions to (Romans 3), it does not follow that Mary must be a sinner based on this verse.

In 1950, Pope Pius XII, in *Munificentissimus Deus,* defined that Mary, *"after the completion of her earthly life was assumed body and soul into the glory of heaven."*

Christ, by his own power, ascended into heaven, but Mary was taken up into Heaven by God.

She didn't do it under her own power. No one knows if she died or not. The majority says she did die by choice in imitation of her Son and Savior.

Besides Enoch, Elijah and perhaps Moses, other bodily assumptions are mentioned in Holy Writ: *"The tombs also were opened, and many bodies of the saints who had fallen asleep were raised, and coming out of the tombs after his resurrection they went into the holy city and appeared to many."* (Matthew 27:52-53)

One cannot argue that Mary's bodily assumption is impossible.

The woman clothed with the sun in the (Apocalypse 12:1) can be interpreted to be Mary. In this verse, we see the woman described with a head and feet, which implies a body. She also has a crown of twelve stars implying that she is a queen.

The woman can also be interpreted to be the Church but since the other figures in the Apocalypse represent specific persons such as the dragon who is Satan and the beast who is the antichrist, then it would follow that the woman could be interpreted as Mary.

There is also the fact that the entire history of the Church has recognized that Mary was taken into Heaven with her body. There is more history to confirm this fact than the Immaculate Conception itself.

Relics of saints are highly prized especially the bones, hair, teeth, etc. There are body relics of every major saint except Mary, who was the greatest human person (Christ was the Divine Person).

Cities and churches boast about the relics of their particular saints but none boast about Mary's. The reason for this is that the faithful have always known that there are none with Mary since her body was taken up.

When we look at the Ark of the Covenant of the Old Testament in reference to Mary of the New Testament, we see that she is the Ark of the New Covenant.

The Old Testament Ark carried the Word of God in the Ten Commandments, the bread of heaven called manna, the staff of Aaron which symbolized the high priesthood.

Mary carried the Word of God in the person of Jesus, who is the true Bread from Heaven, and the high priest.

The Old Testament Ark was made of incorruptible wood, and Mary is incorrupt.

David said, *"How can the ark of the Lord come to me?"* (II Sam 6:9) and Elizabeth said, *"why is this granted to me, that the mother of my Lord should come to me?"*

David danced before the Lord because of the ark (II Sam 6:12-14) and the babe John the Baptist in Elizabeth's womb leaped when approached by Mary. (Luke 1:41)

Just as the Old Testament Ark was overshadowed by the glory of the Lord in (Exodus 40:34-35), so too, Mary was overshadowed by the Holy Ghost in (Luke 1:35).

It is no coincidence that Luke wrote about Mary as the New Ark of the Covenant. He drew from the same books of the Old Testament.

St John's says in his Apocalypse that he sees the Ark of the Covenant in the temple of God in (Apoc. 11:19), and the very next verse describes a *"woman clothed with the sun, with the moon under her feet, and upon her head a crown of twelve stars."*

No doubt, St John is seeing Mary and is saying that she is the Ark of the New Covenant.

The whole Book is about Christ and his triumph over Satan and his wickedness over the earth. It was Mary that brought us our Lord and Savior, and through her, Christ conquers and reigns.

Since the Immaculate Conception and Assumption are not explicit in Scripture, heretics conclude that the doctrines are false.

This comes from the anti-historical, anti-Scriptural, and anti-logical doctrine of Sola Scriptura, or the Protestant *"Bible only"* doctrine.

The Catholic Church was commissioned by Christ to teach all nations and to teach them infallibly—guided, as he promised, by the Holy Spirit until the end of the world (John 14:26, 16:13).

The mere fact that the Church teaches that something is definitely true is a guarantee that it is true (Matt. 18:17-18, 28:18-20, Luke 10:16, 1 Tim. 3:15).

Heretics will, of course, disagree with this position, but the point is made that the Ever Virgin Mary is immaculate *"without sin"* using Scripture and logic to do so.

8. The Best Bible Translations and Why in a Nutshell

There are basically two types of Bible translations, formal equivalence and dynamic equivalence.

Dynamic equivalence means translating the thought process of each word or sentence, or thought-for-thought. The problem with this way of translating may come from the bias of the translator. Many different meanings, ideas or thoughts can come under certain words and sentences. The bias may be in the form of culture or theology, which may give way to extremely false translation.

Formal equivalence is the literal word for word translation. Its only downfall is direct mistranslation, which may include inclusive language.

Then there is the issue of footnotes and commentaries, which range from extremely modernist or liberal based on biased theologies to very accurate based on historic and logical affirmation.

Two examples of popular but bad Bibles

The so-called Catholic NAB or New American Bible uses the formal equivalence. Due to the modernism of its translators, the footnotes include clever but radically altered interpretations from the historical record.

For instance, it claims the author of Matthew may not be Matthew and that he borrowed as a source the Gospel of Mark.

If this were true, then Matthew wouldn't truly be inspired but rather a plagiarized work. The NAB charges the Gospels as contradicting one another in reality rather than just in appearance.

The NAB implies some readings are fraudulent and that Christ was sometimes mistaken. You can find all this and much more in the NAB's footnotes in the Gospel of Matthew alone, not to mention the whole of Scripture. The NAB is so bad that it would not at all be excessive to call it blasphemous. It's not surprising that Paul VI approved it.

The popular NIV or New International Version uses both types. Because this translation is biased against Catholicism, you get direct and intentional mistranslation with words such as tradition.

Since anti-Catholics hate the traditions of Catholicism, each time the Greek *paradosis* or tradition is used in the Bible in a good way such as (Second Thessalonians 2:15), the NIV translates it *"teachings"* with a footnote that it can be rendered tradition. However, when the *paradosis* refers to bad traditions as found in (Mark 7:8-9), the NIV then correctly translates it tradition.

The commentary found in the NIV is radically biased. For instance, (I Peter 3:21) states quite clearly baptism saves. The anti-Catholic translators footnote that Baptism doesn't really save but only symbolizes.

In other words, the Bible doesn't really mean what it states. The Catholic doctrine of Baptism teaches that water actually does what it symbolizes which is saving the soul by washing it away of sin and Peter is teaching the Catholic doctrine precisely.

Many other Bibles have inclusive language and most have many mistranslations.

As with all Protestant versions of the Bible, many Scriptures are intentionally left out.

Imagine if you will a group of churches that rejected certain books in the Bible such as Genesis, Numbers, Job, as not being the Scriptures or Word of God, because they were considered problematic either historically or theologically.

Yet, this is precisely what the Protestants did with the Christian Bible. They rejected the Old Testament deuterocanonical books of Tobit, Judith, Wisdom (of Solomon), Sirach, Baruch, First and Second Maccabees, including parts of Esther and Daniel. Protestants refer to these books as apocrypha. Actually, there is a difference between the apocrypha and the deuterocanonicals.

There are several reasons given by Protestants as to why these books should not be considered canonical, but all such reasons are either false, illogical, and without any merit.

One such reason given is the books are not found in the Hebrew Bible and were rejected by the Jews at the Council of Javneh (Jamnia) in 90 AD. Why this reason is given is puzzling since the Jewish council has no authority whatsoever. It also rejects Christ, all the New Testaments writings, and anything that has to do with the Gentiles.

While it is a fact that the Hebrew Bible does not contain the deuterocanonical books, the Septuagint Bible most certainly contains them and this was the version used by Christ and the Apostles. Even in the Gospels (Mark 7:6-8), Christ quotes from Isaiah found only in the Septuagint version.

As a matter of fact, two-thirds of the Old Testament passages quoted in the New Testament come from the Septuagint.

This fact also squashes any argument that would accuse the Catholic Church of adding these books in the Bible. St Athanasius of the fourth century was the first to give the list of all the books in both the Old and New Testaments that we have today.

Considering also that the first Bible with the 27 books of the New Testament was first given in Rome in 380 by the authority of the Roman Pontiff.

This doesn't mean that the books are Scripture based on the authority of the Catholic Church since they are the Scriptures regardless. However, it took the authority of the Catholic Church to discern them in order that the world can be sure.

In other words, it took an authority outside of Scripture that must be infallible or else the Canon of Scripture itself would not be. Prior to the 380 AD Roman Council, there was no set Canon of Scripture. In other words, there was no Bible. What constituted the Word of God was up for grabs.

Just because the Church existed with conflicting lists of Scripture before 380 AD also doesn't mean that one has the right to reject the deuterocanonicals. Some New Testament books were also not always considered Scriptural such as the books Hebrews and the Apocalypse. Therefore, this excuse cannot be logically used with the deuterocanonical books.

The Divine inspiration of Scripture did not provide the list of Scriptures and even if it did, one could not be sure if they were actually the Scriptures.

The Koran or Quran claims that all its books are the Word of God but does that make it so? Of course not. Christ would need to set up an infallible authority to not only to give the Canon but also to provide the limits on interpretation or else the Word of God is only as good as the one interpreting it.

The infallible Word of God would not be very useful if you didn't know the infallible interpretation of it or at least the limit thereof.

Funny thing is, without realizing it Protestants have accepted the infallible authority of the Catholic Church by accepting their Bibles, as the Canon was determined for the exception of the books mentioned.

This moves us to the next point used as an excuse not to include the deuterocanonicals, which is that they don't claim to be Scripture. The problem with this excuse is that neither do many Scriptural books. Should we toss them out also?

The books Sirach and II Maccabees seem to deny they are Scriptural but so does St. Paul in (I Corinthians 7:12 and 7:40). Should we throw-out First Corinthians too?

Finally, some Protestants will say that the deuterocanonicals have errors. For instance, the books of Judith and Tobit are historically and geographically erroneous. The author of Tobit goes out of his way to let us know his story is fictional, but the Church accepts the stories of God for their theological and moral truths based on what the author is asserting. The Word of God may tell us truths apart from the historical record, and it is the Word of God just the same.

Some Protestants bring up the fact that Judith and the angel Rafael lie and God would be condoning immorality if these books are Scriptural. However, God accepts some deception as praiseworthy under certain circumstances provided that it is contrary to the deception unto sin, such as the Hebrew midwives lying to Pharaoh about the birth of Moses or even Christ saying that He knows not the Day.

Other examples would include the saints that have deceived the government when it came to promoting the Faith and to distribute the sacraments under anti-Catholic law as it did in England, Japan, Mexico, and many other places.

Chapter 12 in Second Maccabees most clearly shows the doctrine of Purgatory. Of course, most Protestants would reject this book since their systematic theology won't allow for the doctrine of Purgatory.

But hey, if you don't like the theology of a certain book in the Bible because it doesn't line up with your theology, then just toss it out right?

Luther hated the New Testament book James because it says man is not justified by faith alone but by faith and works and this did not square up with his theology.

Others just twist the second verse of James to mean something different from what it actually states because they know throwing out James would be wrong, but then you're back to the problem that God's Word is only as good as the one interpreting it.

Be that as it may, some deuterocanonicals have nothing to be answered for and yet they are still rejected. The reason for this deletion is these books are profoundly Catholic. This is not what Protestants will say. They use the other excuses, but ultimately it comes down to authority.

While there are many good bibles without the deuterocanonicals, such as the KJV, NKJV, and the RSV, why not use the Bible with the same authority that gave us what we have? Of course, the consequences would be devastating for some of those who did.

With all this is in mind, two Bibles stand out as the best translated, best-footnoted, best commentary, and best readable.

While there is no such thing as the perfectly translated English Bible, the Douay-Rheims is the most accurate, and the RSV-CE is the best readable. Both should be used in Bible study and prayerful reading.

The Douay is the only Bible to get two very important verses translated correctly into English.

In (Genesis 3:15), the first prophecy of Our Lord and Lady is told. All Bibles but one says *"HE"* will crush the head of Satan. However, this is a false translation.

The historic rendering of this Hebrew pronoun *"hu"* has always and should be rendered *"SHE,"* because the *"woman"* and not the "seed" is the antecedent of *"hu."* This follows the context, because (Gen 3:15) says the enmity is between the "woman" and *"Satan",* then it says, between her *"seed"* and Satan's *"seed."*

If you read the Hebrew pronoun as *"he"* crushing the head of *"Satan"* then you have misplaced the context of who has enmity with whom. *"She"* will crush the head since she was the object that follows and the one who was said to have enmity with *"Satan."* We know of course that it is because of her *"seed"* that she does this.

The next verse is (Luke 1:28). The angel Gabriel addresses Mary as *kecharitomene.* The Douay translates this word as it was translated in Latin. *"Hail, full of grace."* It is not a transliteration.

All other Bibles give a variation of *"Rejoice, O highly favored."* This translation from the Greek lacks what God was conveying to Mary. The Greek is indicating a permanent perfection of favor or grace of a singular kind, not just highly favored. Several saints in Scripture are highly favored, but none are perfectly and permanently favored of a singularly kind and this is what *kecharitomene* means. It is a title and a description. *"Hail, Full of Grace"* nails it down.

All the other Bibles take away from Mary what God has told us about her in these two verses. Therefore, only one Bible gives the greatest glory to God by rightly translating these two verses.

Though the Douay is in the older English making it more difficult to read, the RSV-CE helps when using in prayerful study.

9. The Rapture Heresy in a Nutshell

People all over America are talking about the 'Rapture.' A new series of best selling books *'Left Behind'* exposes this relatively new doctrine. Jack Van Impe preaches it on every one of his TV programs.

What is this Rapture, and is it in the Bible?

The teaching first appeared in the 1800's from John Nelson Darby (Scottish Dispensationalist) and transferred by CI Scofield into his "Scofield Reference Bible." Prior to the 1800's no one claiming Christianity ever heard of this doctrine.

Many psuedo-Christians or heretics use verses such as (I Thess. 4:13-17), when talking about the Rapture, meaning the Church will be taken up with God in the sky before the Great Tribulation and before a thousand-year reign of Christ on earth known as the pre-millennial view or millenarianism. You may have seen bumper stickers with *'In Case of Rapture, this Car will be Unmanned."*

Dr. David Jeremiah on his radio program *'Turning Point'* explains, *"that we should be looking for Christ instead of the antichrist, for the Rapture will happen first, and then the antichrist will rise for the Great Tribulation. The Faithful will not have to endure the Great Tribulation."*

Dr. Jeremiah uses (II Thess. 2:7-8) to show why he believes the Rapture happens before the Tribulation. It says, *"...But the one who restrains is to do so only for the present, until he removed from the scene. And then the lawless one will be revealed."*

According to Dr. Jeremiah, *"the one who restrains is the Holy Spirit and since the church cannot be with out the Holy Spirit then the Rapture happens with the removal of the restraining one.* " Dr. David Reagan on his radio program *'Christ in Prophecy'* says somewhat the same thing. Dr. Reagan believes the restraining one is the Church.

Dr. Jeremiah, also reasons that we will not be around for the Tribulation because nowhere in the Bible explains how we should go through it.

There are other passages that seem to illustrate a pre-tribulational Rapture. (Matt. 24:40-41) states, *"Two men will be out in the field, one will be taken, and one will be left."*

(Luke 17:34-35) gives this account, *"I tell you, on that night there will be two people in one bed: one will be taken, the other left."*

(I Thess. 4:13-17) has it best stating, *"For the Lord himself, with a word of command, with the voice of an archangel and with the trumpet of God, will come down from heaven, and the dead in Christ will rise first. Then we who are alive, who are left, will be caught up together with them in the clouds to meet the Lord in the air. Thus we shall always be with the Lord."* ('Will be caught up' is Rapiemur in Latin, which we get the word 'Rapture.')

What are we to make of all this? First, we must be aware that there are many different forms of writing in Holy Scripture. These are called literary genres. They are easily understood when they are read within the culture of the time. The cause of the confusion is when we take a genre of a different culture from another time and place it within the same context of the present culture.

Apocalyptic writing such as the books of Daniel and Revelation is one literary genre common among the ancient Semites. It is filled with strange illusions, bizarre images and numbers that have symbolic meaning.

There are other genres used in Scripture such as the parable, the allegory, and the historical novel. In each literary form, the writer presents but not necessarily asserts the message of God. It is what the writer meant to assert that we must find out. With this in mind, Holy Scripture should be read within the historic context and living Tradition of the Church.

If this is not done, then the interpretations will vary with every whim and best guess of the reader and will ultimately end with denying the very Word of God. Scripture itself warns of traditions of men that will nullify the Word of God.

It is interesting to note that immediately after the paragraph used to proof text the Rapture theology, is found the very Scriptures that tell us about Sacred Tradition. (II Thess. 2:15) *"Therefore, brothers, stand firm and hold fast to the traditions that you were taught, either by an oral statement or by a letter of ours."*

What about those passages of Scripture that seem to prove the Rapture?

One should ask how the early Church fathers interpreted these passages. Do other passages in Scripture clearly contradict those interpretations?

Without reading them in its historical and biblical context in accord to Church teaching, would be going against what Scripture itself says. As St. Peter warns, *"Know this first of all, that there is no prophecy of Scripture that is a matter of personal interpretation"*(II Peter 1:20) and *"In them there are some things hard to understand that the unlearned and unstable distort to their own destruction, just as they do the other scriptures."*(II Peter 3:16)

Though, many saints have preached a literal thousand-year reign of Christ on earth or millenarianism, never has there been taught this idea of the pre-tribulational Rapture. Scottish

Dispensationalists invented this doctrine less than two hundred years ago and it has since become an American phenomenon.

When investigating the Rapture theology, several problems immediately arise.

In the foundation verse for the Rapture (I Thess. 4:15-17), we see that this Rapture happens with the coming of the Lord, *"for we who are alive, who are left until the coming of the Lord, ... Then we who are alive, who are left, will be caught up."*

In (Matthew 24:29-31) and (Mark 13:24-27), we see that when Christ comes again it is immediately after the Great Tribulation. The psuedo-Christian heretic would have to conclude two second-comings of Christ to keep from contradicting these two passages, and particularly (II Thess. 2:7-8).

On his TV program JVI Presents, Jack Van Impe denies two second-comings. He reasons that the Rapture happens when the Lord appears in the sky but doesn't actually make His Second-Coming.

Since Van Impe uses (I Thess 4) to prove his position, he must conclude that very passage that says the *"coming of the Lord"* is not really the coming of the Lord because that must come later.

Also, the appearance of the Lord in the sky is precisely how Holy Scripture describes the Second Coming. See (Act 1:11).

The fact is the pre-tribulational rapture theorist must believe in two second-comings even if they refuse to acknowledge it as so. Two second-comings is not the historical Christian belief.

Jack Van Impe uses the historical belief in millenarianism to show why the Rapture should be believed. He also misrepresents Catholicism by using her books to show how the Catholic Church also believes in a pre-tribulational Rapture. Unfortunately, he reads into what he wants to see without looking at the whole picture.

Those verses found in (I Thess. 4) that speak of being *"caught up"* is simply speaking about the resurrection of the body for us all on the last day. It is a Christian dogma. As a matter of fact, on that same day the damned will find themselves being *"caught down"* in the same manner.

(Matthew 24:40), *"One will be taken; and one will be left,"* was fulfilled during the destruction of Jerusalem in 70 AD. This whole chapter is on that event which serves as a prototype, or prefigure of the end of time. Look at this verse in light of the next chapter where Christ said he would separate the sheep from the goats. The sheep (Faithful) will be taken and caught up with their bodies, and the goats (unfaithful) will be left and taken down to hell in their bodies. This is the plain explanation of those passages.

In (II Thess. 2:7), the restraining one might be referring to the hierarchy of the Church or perhaps it is St Michael. There is absolutely no reason to believe it is the Holy Spirit or the Church, unless of course you're trying to make it fit into a new theology.

St. Paul writes as if the Thessalonians know what or who it is. No one knows for sure. It is important to know that whatever or whoever it is will be taken out and the antichrist will rise.

Dr. Jeremiah said Scripture doesn't say how we should go through the Great Tribulation and reasons that we must be taken up before it happens.

However, (Matthew 10:22, 24:13) states he who endures and perseveres to the end will be saved. St. Matthew is stating quite emphatically that the Faithful might have to suffer greatly as it goes through the Great Tribulation.

(Hebrews 11:32-40, 12:1-13) is clearly saying that the Faithful may and will have to suffer greatly.

St. Peter, who holds the primacy in the hierarchy, in (I Peter 1:3-9, 2:18-25, 3:13-17, 4:1) speaks about suffering while (Matthew 10:16-18) warns us of the coming persecutions.

Dr. David Jeremiah, Dr. Dave Reagan, Jack Van Impe, Hal Lindsey, Jerry Jenkins, Tim LaHaye and all those like them who profess a pre-tribulational Rapture are the very false teachers St. Peter warns us against. (II Peter 2:1)

As for the Rapture, our focus is on the coming of the Lord but this will be His Second Coming and we are not thinking about getting out of here before the Great Tribulation for we are now going through it.

The number seven represents completeness or wholeness and is erroneous to believe that seven years must be a literal seven rather than a complete and whole time of trial. The expression of a thousand years also represents a round number of a long period of time. It is not to be taken as a literal one thousand years.

One could argue that a thousand years is a single day since Scripture also has it a thousand years is as one day to the Lord. (II Peter 3:8) The point is there are other ways to view the thousand years of peace rather than the pre-millennialists or millenarianists. Pope Pius XII declared this position couldn't be safely held.

As for the Second Coming of our Lord, we will be judged as we live since that day will usher in the Final Judgment.

We hold fast to Sacred Scripture and Sacred Tradition, and profess in the Apostles' Creed, *"He will come again to judge the living and the dead."* On that day, the same Apostles' Creed continues with *"I believe in... the resurrection of the body."*

The resurrection of the bodies to the souls of the Faithful is the true Rapture and it happens on the last day of time as we know it when we will enter the age of ages.

10. The History of Churches in a Nutshell

Listed below are 25 religions that claim to follow Jesus Christ.

These historical facts will have the description of the name, place, founder, and year of each denomination. The last Church is the one founded by Christ Himself.

1. The Eastern Orthodox Churches were founded in North Africa, by the Patriarch of Constantinople Michael Cerularius during the middle 11ᵗʰ century. After the great schism, all the churches of the East split nationally since the pope was no longer recognized as the visible head of the Church.

2. The Lutheran Church was founded in Germany by Martin Luther, an ex-monk of the Roman Catholic Church, in 1521.

3. The Mennonite Churches were founded in Switzerland by Menno Simons, an ex-Catholic priest, in 1525.

4. The Church of England (Anglican) was founded by King Henry VIII, an ex-Catholic defender of the Faith in 1534.

5. The Presbyterian Churches were founded in Scotland by John Knox, an ex-Catholic priest, in 1560. The teachings come from the notorious Protestant Reformer John Calvin.

6. The Congregational Churches were founded in Holland by Robert Brown in 1583.

7. The Baptist Churches, now split into 30 sects with the Baptist name, were founded in Amsterdam by founder John Smyth in 1609.

8. The Unitarian Church was founded in London by John Biddle in 1645.

9. The Quaker Churches were founded in England by George Fox in 1647.

10. The Methodist Churches were founded in England by John and Charles Wesley, in 1739.

11. The Universalists were founded in New Jersey by John Murray in 1770.

12. The Episcopal Church was founded in America by Anglican colonists who elected Samuel Seabury as the first bishop in 1783.

13. The Evangelical Church was founded in Pennsylvania by Jacob Albright in 1803.

14. The Church of Latter Day Saints (Mormon) was founded in Palmyra, New York by Joseph Smith in 1829.

15. The Seventh Day Adventist Church was founded in New York by William Miller in 1831.

16. The Christian Churches, (Disciples of Christ and Church of Christ), were founded in Kentucky by Barton Stone, and Thomas and Alexander Campbell in 1832.

17. The Salvation Army was founded in London by William Booth in 1865.

18. Kingdom Hall of the Jehovah Witnesses was founded in Pittsburgh by Charles Taze Russell in 1870, known as the "Russellites, or Millennial Dawn People." Judge Rutherford, his successor, took over the movement in 1916 in Brooklyn, New York and began calling themselves Jehovah Witnesses a few years later.

19. The Christian Scientist Church was founded in Massachusetts by Mary Baker Eddy in 1879.

20. The Church of God is one of over 200 sects founded in Tennessee by A. J. Tomlinson in 1880. The Church of the Nazarene is one of these sects founded from the Union at General Assembly in 1919. The Evangelical Reformed Church came from the same Union at General Assembly in 1934.

21. Messianic Judaism was founded in America. Though the roots can be traced to the late 1900's in Europe up to the Boston Conference of the Messianic Council in 1901, the first Hebrew Christian Synagogue was formed in Philadelphia by John Zacker in 1922. However, out from this sect of Hebrew Christianity, the modern form of Messianic Judaism as we have it today originated in 1973 by Martin Chernoff. This group does not refer to itself as Christian and uses the original Hebrew name of Jesus Christ, Yeshua Messiah.

22. The Pentecostal Churches, which have thousands of sects, were originally founded in America by ex- Baptists and Methodists, in the early 20th century. The Assembly of God is one of those thousands of Pentecostal sects started in Arkansas by the General Assembly in 1914.

23. The United Church of Christ was founded in Oberlin, Ohio by a merger of the Congregational Christian Churches and the Evangelical and Reformed Church in 1959.

24. All churches known as Non-Denominational and Charismatic Churches were formed out of the above sects that exploded within the last 25 years in America.

25. The Vatican 2 sect or the Counterfeit Catholic Church was founded in the 1960's during the Second Vatican Council in Rome under antipopes John XXIII and Paul VI. It constitutes the majority and what many think are Catholic Churches. Its head is the antipope Benedict XVI. Its sacraments are invalid and will remain so.

The Roman Catholic Church (which includes Eastern Rites) was founded in the Holy Land by Our Lord and Savior Jesus

Christ on the Apostle Peter (the first Pope) and his faith around 30 AD. This Church is now gone underground due to the Counterfeit Catholic Church.

Christ said that the gates of hell shall not prevail against His Church and that He would be with His Church until the end of time. Only one church can claim to be the Church founded by Christ for it is the only church found in every generation and in every land with the same faith for the past 20+ centuries.

Jesus founded His one holy Catholic Church by and through the Holy Spirit who is its Living Soul.

Mere men founded every other church in history.

Are you going to be faithful and obedient to Jesus by going to and through Him on His terms or attempt to go to Him on man's terms? Those are your only two choices. One is that narrow road (Catholic Church) that leads into Paradise, while the other choice is the wide path (the thousands of man-made non-Catholic churches) that leads to destruction!

Everybody claims to go by the Holy Bible but the Catholic Church gave us the Holy Bible in 380 AD and follows the historical interpretation of it.

Jesus purposely did not give His Church a name for any false church could usurp that name. Instead, He let men give His Church the name while He gave us the 4 marks to find it. His Church is one (united), holy (teachings come from Christ), catholic (universal), and apostolic (comes down to us from the Apostles).

Do you stay in a church just because you were brought up there, or because you like the atmosphere or because of family and friends? Is it because you are afraid of rejection due to what your family and friends might think or say? Jesus said that he did not come to bring peace but the sword, one that may divide even family members. (Matt. 10:34)

Don't judge the Catholic Church by its unholy members as you would not judge Christ and His Apostles by Judas Iscariot. Rather, judge the Catholic Church from its Saints who believed and followed Christ as they give the example of real Christianity.

Instead of living in the 20th and 21st centuries, lets suppose you lived in the 9th and 10th centuries. What church would you attend? Since you believe the Catholic Church is a false church then you would not attend it but the problem is your only other choices would be the Paulicians, and the Nestorians. The Montanists already died out. The several Cathar sects such as the Albigenses and Waldenses came centuries later.

You also could not argue the Catholic Church was different then because it has exactly the same doctrines and practices today as it did then.

If you think the Catholic Church is not Christ's Church then you cannot possibly explain how the Catholic Church was the only Christian Church through all of those centuries with the same teachings while no other church existed except those with extreme heretical beliefs just mentioned.

If you do not believe the Catholic Church is the church Christ founded then you must conclude that Jesus was a liar since his church did not exist in certain periods of history.

You also could not argue that there was an invisible church meaning there were Christians in the Catholic Church who actually rejected the teachings of the Catholic Church while believing the same things Protestants, Evangelicals, and Fundamentalists. Those non-Catholic beliefs did not exist for another 5 centuries later, coming from men reinventing religion based on their own personal interpretation of Scriptures.

Catholics hold fast to the faith that was delivered to them from the beginning and calls to mind the warning of St. Paul, *"But even if we, or an angel from heaven, should preach to you a gospel contrary to that which we preached to you, let him be accursed. As we have said before, so now I say again, if any one is preaching to you a gospel contrary to that which you received, let him be accursed.* "(Galatians 1:8-9)

The Protestant Revolt gave us another gospel contrary to that of 1500 yrs of Christianity while claiming to be true Christianity. For those Revolters according to St. Paul under the inspiration of the Holy Spirit, *"let him be accursed."*

Will you ignore history and follow a novel religion that has a gospel that was not delivered from the beginning? The answer to this question depends on your sincerity to follow Jesus who is the Truth.

11. Catholic or Not

(A Catechism on Sedevacantism in a Nutshell)

What is Sedevacantism?

Sedevacantism is a position held by Catholics who are holding fast to the traditional Catholic Faith. Sedevacantism comes from the Latin - Sede Vacant (the Chair is Vacant). Those Catholics who hold this position are called sedevacantists.

What do Sedevacantists believe?

Sedevacantists believe the Chair of Peter or the Papacy is currently vacant. All those who claim to be pope are actually antipopes.

What is an antipope?

An antipope is anyone who claims to be pope but is not actually the pope.

Why do Sedevacantists believe the current *"pope"* is actually an antipope?

Sedevacantists believe that a true pope must hold the Catholic Faith and do not believe the current *"pope"* Benedict XVI is a Catholic. They also do not believe other requirements have been fulfilled by the current *"pope."*

What are the requirements to be pope?

The first requirement is to be a man. The second requirement is a valid election, although this is not absolute. The third requirement is the formal consent of the elected. The fourth requirement (only if needed) is to ordain the elected a priest and consecrate him bishop. The fifth requirement is to hold fast to Catholic teachings after one becomes a pope.

Since the current *"pope"* claims to be Catholic, what is the requirement to be Catholic?

To be a Catholic, one must believe in all the teachings of the Church and not knowingly reject any of them, and practice the faith under the laws of God and the Church. He must also acknowledge legitimate authority and not knowingly reject this authority. Anyone who claims to be a Catholic, but knowingly does not believe, practice and follow the Catholic faith is automatically anathematized. He is at that point, no longer Catholic.

What does anathematize mean?

Anathematize (root word – anathema) means to be cut off or to be accursed. To be excommunicated is another common name for anathema. There is either an automatic anathema or declared anathema attached to every heretic and schismatic. Everyone who is anathematized is no longer a Catholic but rather becomes a non-Catholic heretic or schismatic.

What is a heretic?

A heretic is any Baptized person who knowingly rejects a Catholic teaching or believes in a heresy, which is a false belief.

What is a schismatic?

A schismatic is any Baptized person who knowingly refuses to be in unity with the Church. This can happen by refusing to conform one's self to lawful authority or lawful authoritative pronouncements.

Who do sedevacantists believe was the last true pope?

It depends on which sedevacantist you ask. The informed Catholic sedevacantist believes it was Pope Pius XII. Some falsely believe Cardinal Siri was elected after Pope Pius XII. Some falsely believe it was Paul VI.

Is there a true pope out there that is not known to the public?

It is possible that there is a true pope not known, but is not a probable proposition.

Is sedevacantism possible?

Sedevacantism happens every time a pope dies. The Chair of Peter is vacant until another pope is elected. This is called the period of interregnum. Some have argued that there must be a pope within 50 years, but the Church has never declared it. Therefore, it is only the opinion of some that it is an impossible position, and they can only give their fallible opinions why they think it is an impossible position. Only the Magisterium can make that determination, and it has never done so.

Didn't the First Vatican Council say there would always be pope?

No, the First Vatican Council said the office of papacy is perpetual. This does not mean that there will always be a pope. The Chair of Peter has been vacant for long periods of time before, though never like it has been now.

Will there ever be a new pope?

A future election by ordinary means is not possible. A future election by extraordinary means is possible or God Himself intervenes and supernaturally gives us a pope.

Doesn't that make the Church wrong at the First Vatican Council since the Chair of Peter is no longer perpetual?

No, the Chair of Peter is always in place. The First Vatican Council did not say the Chair would always be filled. The principle was what the First Vatican Council was addressing, since it was denied that Peter was ever to have successors. The fact is Peter had successors all the way to Pope Pius XII. Therefore, the principle of perpetual succession is in place.

Can the Church survive without a pope? Has it done so before?

The Church has now survived about 50 years without a pope. The Church has survived 3 and half years in the past as the longest period. It survives each time a pope dies because the Church was not built upon the papacy but on the faith of the first pope. It is the Faith that makes up the Faithful. The Holy Catholic Church is the Faithful who keep the faith.

How can the Church survive without a pope?

It survives by the Grace of God who keeps it alive through the power of the Holy Ghost. As long as one person holds the faith the Catholic Church is alive on earth.

How does Christ tell us to be faithful to Him?

Christ told us to be perfect, to obey the Commandments, to listen to those whom He sent. He told us to reject false teachers, and to listen to His Church.

How can we listen to the Church if there is no pope?

We live in humility and listen to all the teachings handed down by all the true popes. We do not listen to false teachers as Christ said to reject them. Anyone who teaches contrary to any of the teachings handed down is a false teacher. Christ forewarned us of the many of them that will come in the last days. The last five claimants to the papacy have clearly and unambigucusly taught contrary to the historic Catholic Faith. Therefore, it is not possible for any of them to be true popes.

Why does Christ forewarn of false teachers?

Christ warned us of false teachers because they can lead you into hell. Heresy separates us from Christ and anyone who claims to teach in the name of Christ or His Church could fool you into believing heresy that leads you to hell. This is why an anti-pope can be so dangerous because he could teach contrary to Catholic doctrine and fool you into believing that his heresy is really Catholic. This is precisely what has been happening for the past 50 years.

What else do the Scriptures say?

There will be a time when men will not listen to the truth and that God's people will be associated with the harlot and to come out.

Check out Peter's Epistles...

Can a Catholic reject some small teaching or practice and still be considered a Catholic?

A Catholic cannot be a Catholic and knowingly reject any Catholic teaching at the same time.

Define Catholic teaching.

A Catholic teaching is any teaching that comes from Christ and the Apostles, the Church and specifically the pope when that teaching concerns our salvation and is given to the whole Church.

What if a true pope knowingly rejects Catholic teaching?

If a true pope knowingly rejects Catholic teaching, he would at once cease to be a Catholic and therefore cease to be pope and would lose all jurisdiction. One cannot be Head of the Church if he is not a member of the Church.

Can a man who knowingly rejects Catholic teaching be elected pope?

A man who knowingly rejects Catholic teaching can be elected pope but must reject his error and hold the faith to actually be pope after his election or else the man would not be a Catholic and therefore not pope.

How is it possible to identify the true Church if a false Church usurps the name?

The Catholic Church instituted by Christ has two particular marks not found in any other church. In one of these particular marks *"holy"* is found...infallibility and indefectibility. The other mark *"Apostolic"* is found historicity. A false Church like the Vatican 2 Church is not holy or apostolic. See Appendix to see how the Vatican 2 Church is neither holy nor apostolic.

Our Lord Himself told his Church to remain faithful to Him and to those whom He sends forth provided those whom He sends also remain faithful to Him. Only one Church has done so.

What is infallibility and how does it work? (What does it entail)?

Infallibility is a special chrism or gift of the pope. It means that the pope cannot error in teaching the faithful under certain circumstances. When the pope teaches ex cathedra (from the Chair) meaning as the head of the whole Church to the whole Church anything on faith and morals to be held as truth never to be altered, he is infallible. It is a preventive measure given to him by Christ and the Holy Ghost to prevent heresy (known as the Gates of Hell or Powers of Death) from ever being taught by the Church.

Just as God used fallible men to write the infallible Holy Scriptures, God now uses fallible men to teach the Gospel of the Holy Scriptures infallibly. The Bible would not be completely useful without some interpretations of some passages with some boundaries and limits of interpretations on other passages. The books in the Bible, themselves, have been infallibly determined by the Church to be infallible. It took an infallible authority to tell what the infallible Scriptures are, or else, the Bible itself would not be known. Scriptures are infallible because they are God-breathed, but we would not know what precisely what and which of these God-breathed books are God-breathed without an infallible authority outside of the Bible.

What is indefectibility and how does infallibility effect indefectibility? (Its implications)

Indefectibility means not defected or not able to be defected. Infallibility prevents the Church from being defected. In other words, truth is immutable. The Church can never proclaim or define an untruth. This aspect of indefectibility insures us infallibility.

Once a truth is proclaimed or defined by the Church, that truth is set in stone, so to speak, never to be altered or changed.

The Church is infallible thus it is indefectible. The Church is indefectible thus it is infallible.

What must Catholic sedevacantists believe?

Catholic sedevacantists must believe everything the Church has taught and reject everything that is opposed to it.

Is there such a case that a Catholic could resist or reject something that comes from the Church?

Since the Catholic Faith is immaculate in all her universal teachings, laws and disciplines, there would be no need to do so. However, one could resist or reject any individual, even the Pope, if he were to command one to sin. But the pope can't possibly command one to sin by a universal Church teaching, law, or discipline.

Who can judge a pope if that pope becomes heretical or schismatic?

According to Pope Innocent III and St. Robert Bellarmine, any Catholic can make that judgment.

Again, why must a Catholic hold the position of sedevacantism?

He must hold the position of sedevacantism as a matter of faith, since the Church cannot have a heretical pope nor can the Church teach or practice something harmful as the Vatican 2 church does.

How does the Church fulfill the mark *"one"* now?

The Church fulfills the mark of oneness as it always has; by holding to the faith as it has been defined. Every time a true pope dies, the Church remains one by this means.

What about Christ naming Peter in Matt. 16? Did Christ build the Church on the papacy?

Christ built the Church on Peter and his faith together, but not necessarily the office of Peter. The office is a necessary part of the Church as are the sacraments but the Church wasn't built on them either. Peter's name represented his faith. If Christ built the Church on the office of Peter, then the foundation of the Church is gone every time a pope dies. Without a foundation, there is no church.

Did the last 5 claimants lose their office or did they never have it?

The last 5 claimants never had it for all had defective elections. Had any of them been validly elected, they would have still lost the office. However, none of them were validly elected.

Appendix

The mark of holiness means that all teachings and practices are holy. The Vatican II church has teachings previously condemned with practices previously condemned as unholy. The mark of apostolicity means it comes from the Apostles, which means the particular teachings and practices that came from Vatican II did not come from the Apostles.

Examples of teachings of Vatican II and how they are condemned:

The Vatican II church teaches:

Dogmatic Constitution Lumen Gentium Chapter 2. The people of God

15. "For several reasons the Church recognizes that it is joined to those who, though baptized and so honored with the Christian name, do not profess the faith in its entirety or do not preserve communion under the successor of St. Peter."

Condemned by:

Pope Pius IX, *Amantissimus* (# 3), April 8, 1862: *"There are other, almost countless, proofs drawn from the most trustworthy witnesses which clearly and openly testify with great faith, exactitude, respect and obedience that all who want to belong to the true and only Church of Christ must honor and obey this Apostolic See and the Roman Pontiff."*

And

Pope Leo XIII, *Satis Cognitum* (# 13), June 29, 1896: *"Therefore if a man does not want to be, or to be called, a heretic, let him not*

*strive to please this or that man... but let him hasten before all
things to be in communion with the Roman See."*

The Vatican II Church teaches:

Unitatis Redintegratio (Decree on Ecumenism) 3.

*"It follows that these separated churches and communities as
such, though we believe them to be deficient in some respects,
have by no means been deprived of significance and importance in
the mystery of salvation. For the Spirit of Christ has not refrained
from using them as means of salvation whose efficacy comes from
that fullness of grace and truth which has been entrusted to the
Catholic Church."*

Condemned by:

Pope Leo XIII, *Satis Cognitum* (# 9), June 29, 1896: *"The Church
alone offers to the human race that religion – that state of
absolute perfection – which He wished, as it were, to be
incorporated in it. And it alone supplies those means of salvation
which accord with the ordinary counsels of Providence."*

The Vatican II church teaches:

*Dogmatic Constitution Lumen Gentium Chapter 2. The people of
God*

*16. "But the plan of salvation also embraces those who
acknowledge the Creator, and among these the Muslims are first;
they profess to hold the faith of Abraham and along with us they
worship the one merciful God who will judge mankind on the last
day."*

And

*Nostra aetate (Declaration on the church's relation to non-
Christian religions)*

3. "The Church also looks upon Muslims with respect. They worship the one God living and subsistent, merciful and mighty, creator of heaven and earth, who has spoken to humanity and to whose decrees, even the hidden ones, they seek to submit themselves whole-heartedly, just as Abraham, to whom the Islamic faith readily relates itself, submitted to God...Hence they have regard for the moral life and worship God in prayer, almsgiving and fasting."

Condemned by:

The Most Holy Scriptures – St. John Chapter 8:

[38] I speak of what I have seen with my Father, and you do what you have heard from your father."
[39] They answered him, "Abraham is our father." Jesus said to them, "If you were Abraham's children, you would do what Abraham did,
[40] but now you seek to kill me, a man who has told you the truth which I heard from God; this is not what Abraham did.
[41] You do what your father did." They said to him, "We were not born of fornication; we have one Father, even God."
[42] Jesus said to them, "If God were your Father, you would love me, for I proceeded and came forth from God; I came not of my own accord, but he sent me.
[43] Why do you not understand what I say? It is because you cannot bear to hear my word.
[44] You are of your father the devil, and your will is to do your father's desires. He was a murderer from the beginning, and has nothing to do with the truth, because there is no truth in him. When he lies, he speaks according to his own nature, for he is a liar and the father of lies.
[45] But, because I tell the truth, you do not believe me.

And

Pope Eugene IV, Council of Basel, Session 19, Sept. 7, 1434: *"the abominable sect of Mahomet"*

And

Pope Clement V, Council of Vienne, 1311-1312: *"It is an insult to the holy name and a disgrace to the Christian faith that in certain parts of the world subject to Christian princes where Saracens (i.e., The followers of Islam, also called Muslims) live, sometimes apart, sometimes intermingled with Christians, the Saracen priests, commonly called Zabazala, in their temples or mosques, in which the Saracens meet to adore the infidel Mahomet, loudly invoke and extol his name each day at certain hours from a high place... This brings disrepute on our faith and gives great scandal to the faithful.   These practices cannot be tolerated without displeasing the divine majesty. We therefore, with the sacred council's approval, strictly forbid such practices henceforth in Christian lands. We enjoin on Catholic princes, one and all. They are to forbid expressly the public invocation of the sacrilegious name of Mahomet... Those who presume to act otherwise are to be so chastised by the princes for their irreverence, that others may be deterred from such boldness.*

The Vatican II church teaches:

Dignitatis Humanae (Declaration of religious freedom)

2. *"This Vatican synod declares that the human person has a right to religious freedom. Such freedom consists in this, that all should have such immunity from coercion by individuals, or by groups, or by any human power, that no one should be force to act against his conscience in religious matters, nor prevented from acting according to his conscience, whether in private or in public, within due limits."*

 # 4: "In addition, religious communities are entitled to teach and give witness to their faith publicly in speech and writing without hindrance."

Condemned by:

Pope Gregory XVI, *Mirari Vos* (# 15), Aug. 15, 1832: *"Here We must include that harmful and never sufficiently denounced freedom to publish any writings whatever and disseminate them to the people, which some dare to demand and promote with so great a clamor. We are horrified to see what monstrous doctrines and prodigious errors are disseminated far and wide in countless books, pamphlets, and other writings which, though small in weight, are very great in malice."*

And

Pope Leo XIII, *Libertas* (# 42), June 20, 1888: *"From what has been said it follows that it is quite unlawful to demand, to defend, or to grant unconditional freedom of thought, of speech, or writing, or of worship, as if these were so many rights given by nature of man."*

And

Pope Leo XIII, *Immortale Dei* (# 34), Nov. 1, 1885: *"Thus, Gregory XVI in his encyclical letter Mirari Vos, dated August 15, 1832, inveighed with weighty words against the sophisms which even at his time were being publicly inculcated – namely, that no preference should be shown for any particular form of worship; that it is right for individuals to form their own personal judgments about religion; that each man's conscience is his sole and all-sufficing guide; and that it is lawful for every man to publish his own views, whatever they may be, and even to conspire against the state."*

Examples of practices of the Vatican II church and how they are condemned:

The Vatican II church practices:

Altar girls, female lectors, and female acolytes as in ministers of the Eucharist

Condemned by:

Pope Benedict XIV, *Encyclical,* July 26, 1755: *Allatae Sunt:*
Women Assisting at Mass
Pope Gelasius in his ninth letter (chap. 26) to the bishops of
Lucania condemned the evil practice which had been introduced of
women serving the priest at the celebration of Mass. Since this
abuse had spread to the Greeks, Innocent IV strictly forbade it in
his letter to the bishop of Tusculum: "Women should not dare to
serve at the altar; they should be altogether refused this
ministry." We too have forbidden this practice in the same words
in Our oft-repeated constitution Etsi Pastoralis, sect. 6, no. 21.

And

St. Paul and the Holy Spirit in the (First Letter to the Corinthians
14:33-36) and the (First Letter to Timothy 2:8-15).

12. Christ's Church VS Satan's Churches in a Nutshell

There is a perverse and pervasive belief held by many, who call themselves Christian, that the Church of Christ is the body of true believers, which can and does cross many denominational lines. It is not the denominational or nondenominational church that really matters, but the personal faith of the individuals, and these individuals are the ones who make up the Church of Christ. In other words, the Church of Christ subsists in any particular denomination.

Most all Protestants hold this view as well as the new religion of Rome. The Second Vatican Council actually states this very thing in its dogmatic constitution by stating that the Church of Christ subsists in the Catholic Church explaining that other non-Catholic churches help build up the one Body of Christ in its Decree on Ecumenism.

According to the Bible, this is impossible. Different faiths of Christ do not make up the one Faith of Christ, but this is precisely what most so-called Christians actually believe.

This is a complete falsehood and flatly contradicts the very Bible they all claim to follow. It denies that the Church is the ONE FAITH of Christ. Faith is not just a belief in Christ, for even the demons believe (James 2:19). Demons are not of the one faith of Christ.

Make no mistake about it; any church that professes such a lie is not a Christian church but rather a satanic church that only professes "a" belief in Christ but not "the" belief of Christ.

If this sounds a little over-the-top, then perhaps a re-examining of the evidence is in order.

Satan means adversary. Anything that is contrary to Christ would be satanic. This is why Christ said to Peter, *"Get behind me, Satan! You are a hindrance to me; for you are not on the side of God, but of men."* (Matthew 16:23, Mark 8:33)

The Satanic Church doesn't worship the devil per se, but rather worships against Christ. Any religion that goes against the true religion is, without a doubt, a religion of the devil or a satanic church. Christ said, *"He who is not with me is against me, and he who does not gather with me scatters."* (Matthew 12:30)

Some churches, such as the new religion of Rome, hold that their particular church has the fullness of means of salvation, but that the means of salvation can be found in other denominational churches.

This lie, that the Church of Christ subsists in this or that denomination, is Satanic because it allows each individual to follow his own system of beliefs. It is Satanic because it follows the laws of the devil, *"To each his own,"* which leads to *"Do as thou wilt."*

All roads do not lead to heaven, but only one road and Christ said it was so narrow that few would even find it (Matt. 7:14).

There are others who believe their particular church is the one true church even though their church was founded by some man within the last 500 years.

According to the Bible, this also is impossible, because it denies that the Church Christ founded was infallible and indefectible and would last all days. It presupposes the Church must have died and needed to be rebuilt or resurrected.

The following Scripture passages by themselves will refute through implication why all these things are false beliefs about the Church. They will also demonstrate how these individuals are actually outside of the Church and apart from the very faith of

Christ they claim to hold. Thus their personal faith in Christ then becomes the very stumbling block on which they will fall into condemnation.

May the following Word of God wipe clean this sinister snare of Satan to find the true Church and reject all the clever works of the Devil.

Truth matters or else there would be no point to religion whatsoever. Why practice any religion if it does not matter whether it is true or not?

If one religion is better than another but both are legitimate roads to Heaven, why would anyone practice the most difficult religion if only to have a greater place in Heaven but a greater chance of hell? Would Christ ask us to gamble with our souls?

All roads may lead to Rome but again only one road leads to Heaven.

Comments have been added to many of these verses to hammer down the point; the Church of Christ is one faith, which can only be of one particular church in the world. All other churches, that claim to follow Christ, are in reality merely man-made religions, which have used every lie in the book to reject the one and only true Church Christ founded.

These psuedo-churches usurping the Christian name are truly the most satanic religions of the world.

The one and only road to Heaven is Jesus Christ as He Himself states, *"I am the way, and the truth, and the life; no one comes to the Father, but by me."*(John 14:6)

Christ implies that apart from the truth is apart from the way and life itself. The *"Way"* was how the Church was first known. The Way, Truth, and Life are so linked together, that you cannot have one without the others. You cannot have only one part of Christ. You either have Him totally or not at all.

Jesus replied to Pontius Pilate, *"You say that I am a king. For this I was born, and for this I have come into the world, to bear witness to the truth."*(John 18:37)

Christ bore witness to *"the"* truth. This means truth is not relative. If it is true for you, it must be true for me.

Jesus said he would build His [one] Church and it will never die.

"And I tell you, you are Peter, and on this rock I will build my church, and the gates of hell shall not prevail against it." (Matthew 16:18)

"I am with you all days, even unto the consummation of the world."(Matthew 28:20)

Notice, Christ built a church, not churches. The 20,000 plus denominations and non-denominations today, do not add up to *"a"* church. All have different ways, beliefs, teachings, and practices. They all do not make up a single religious church.

The Church of Christ is the Body of Christ because She is the Bride of Christ.

(Ephesians 5:22-32) *"[22] Wives, be subject to your husbands, as to the Lord. [23] For the husband is the head of the wife as Christ is the head of the church, his body, and is himself its Savior. [24] As the church is subject to Christ, so let wives also be subject in everything to their husbands. [25] Husbands, love your wives, as Christ loved the church and gave himself up for her, [26] that he might sanctify her, having cleansed her by the washing of water with the word, [27] that he might present the church to himself in splendor, without spot or wrinkle or any such thing, that she might be holy and without blemish. [28] Even so husbands should love their wives as their own bodies. He who loves his wife loves himself. [29] For no man ever hates his own flesh, but nourishes and cherishes it, as Christ does the church, [30] because we are members of his body. [31] "For this reason a man shall leave his father and mother and be joined to his wife, and the two shall become one flesh." [32] This mystery is a profound one, and I am saying that it refers to Christ and the church;"*

(Colossians 1:18, 24) *"[18]He is the head of the body, the church; [24] his body, that is, the church,"*

(I Corinthians 6:15) *"Do you not know that your bodies are members of Christ? Shall I therefore take the members of Christ and make them members of a prostitute? Never!"*

(I Corinthians 12:27) *"Now you are the body of Christ and individually members of it."*

(Romans 12:4-5) *"For as in one body we have many members, and all the members do not have the same function, so we, though many, are one body in Christ, and individually members one of another."*

The Church Christ founded is the Way.

(Acts 9:2) *"so that if he found any belonging to the Way"*

(Acts 19:9, 23) *"[9] when some were stubborn and disbelieved, speaking evil of the Way before the congregation [23] About that time there arose no little stir concerning the Way."*

(Acts 24:14, 22) *"[14] that according to the Way, which they call a sect, worship the God of our fathers, believing everything laid down by the law or written in the prophets, [22] But Felix, having a rather accurate knowledge of the Way,"*

If Christ is the Way and the Church is the Way, and the Church is the Body of Christ, then apart from Christ and the Church is apart from Life. Apart from life means apart from salvation, therefore, outside the church there is no salvation.

The Church is Christ's Flock.

"I am the good shepherd; I know my own and my own know me, as the Father knows me and I know the Father; and I lay down my life for the sheep. And I have other sheep, that are not of this fold; I must bring them also, and they will heed my voice. So there shall be one flock, one shepherd."(John 10:14-16)

"Every one who is of the truth hears my voice."(John 18:37)

(I Peter 5:1-4) *"So I exhort the elders among you, as a fellow elder and a witness of the sufferings of Christ as well as a partaker in the glory that is to be revealed. Tend the flock of God that is your charge, not by constraint but willingly, not for shameful gain but eagerly, not as domineering over those in your charge but being examples to the flock. And when the chief Shepherd is manifested you will obtain the unfading crown of glory."*

The Church is *"of the truth"* because it hears the voice of Christ, who is the Head and Shepherd. Again, there is only *"one flock"* not different flocks. Those who are not of the one flock, Christ must bring into the fold. The implication again, is the flock will attain salvation with the *"crown of glory",* but outside the fold there will not be that crown of glory meaning no salvation.

The Church is a visible institution.

"You are the light of the world. A city set on a hill cannot be hid."(Matthew 5:14)

(I Corinthians 12:28) *"And God has appointed in the church first apostles, second prophets, third teachers, then workers of miracles, then healers, helpers, administrators, and speakers in various kinds of tongues."*

(Colossians 1:24-25) *"his body, that is, the church, of which I became a minister according to the divine office"*

The Church is visible or else these passages are meaningless. If there are apostles and they are first, then the rest should follow them because Apostles are leaders, overseers, and the bishops of the Church. They did not appoint themselves but were appointed by Christ Himself or other Apostles after Him. They don't start their own churches (denominations and non-denominations) but spread the one Church already founded.

The Church is the household of God.

(Ephesians 2:19-22) *"So then you are no longer strangers and sojourners, but you are fellow citizens with the saints and members of the household of God, built upon the foundation of the apostles and prophets, Christ Jesus himself being the cornerstone, in whom the whole structure is joined together and grows into a holy temple in the Lord; in whom you also are built into it for a dwelling place of God in the Spirit."*

(I Timothy 3:15) *"you may know how one ought to behave in the household of God, which is the church of the living God."*

Notice, the Church is built upon Christ and the apostles and prophets, not men reinventing religion with a new foundation of enlightened thought such as the Protestant and Evangelical Reformers who started their own churches based on what they thought the church should be. Sola Scriptura (Bible Alone) is the myth, which became the justification to reject the foundation of the Apostles, and create a new foundation and just call it the foundation of the Apostles. Modernism is the enlightened thought of the new religion of Rome, which replaced historic Christianity and usurped the Catholic name.

The Church is the household of Faith.

(Galatians 6:10) *"So then, as we have opportunity, let us do good to all men, and especially to those who are of the household of faith."*

The Church equals Faith. If you have *"the"* Faith, you are of *"the"* Church.

The Church is the one Faith.

(Ephesians 4:4-6) *"There is one body and one Spirit, just as you were called to the one hope that belongs to your call, one Lord, one faith, one baptism, one God and Father of us all, who is above all and through all and in all."*

(I Timothy 6:20-21) *"O Timothy, guard what has been entrusted to you. Avoid the godless chatter and contradictions of what is falsely called knowledge, for by professing it some have missed the mark as regards the faith. Grace be with you."*

(Jude 1:20) *"But you, beloved, build yourselves up on your most holy faith; pray in the Holy Spirit;"*

Since there is only one Lord, it only follows that there is only one Faith. The Church is the Body of Christ. It equals the Faith, which equals the Way, the Truth, and the Life.

The Church has true authority.

"...tell it to the church; and if he refuses to listen even to the church, let him be to you as a Gentile and a tax collector. Truly, I say to you, whatever you bind on earth shall be bound in heaven, and whatever you loose on earth shall be loosed in heaven." (Matthew 18: 17-18)

(Galatians 1:8) *"But even if we, or an angel from heaven, should preach to you a gospel contrary to that which we preached to you, let him be accursed (anathema or cut-off)."*

(Titus 2:15) *"Declare these things; exhort and reprove with all authority. Let no one disregard you."*

If one has a disagreement about something of the Faith, which Church does he take it to? If the Faith is the Church, then there must be someone whom has the authority in the Church to say so. This someone is the one who has the authority to bind and loose. He is the one whom has the authority to anathematize. Although several persons could make certain decisions in the Church, it ultimately must come down to one person in the end. But the authority cannot be rejected or else you will automatically be cut-off from the Way. Thus, the rejection of this authority will be the rejection of salvation. ***"Whoever hears you, hears me; and whoever rejects you, rejects me,"*** says the Lord Jesus. (Luke 10:16)

The Church is immaculate and has no flaws or defections.

(Ephesians 5:25-27) *"Christ loved the church and gave himself up for her, that he might sanctify her, having cleansed her by the washing of water with the word, that he might present the church to himself in splendor, without spot or wrinkle or any such thing, that she might be holy and without blemish."*

This demonstrates how one cannot complain about anything the Church teaches or practices or else the implication would be the Church is not a spotless Bride, but a whore. He who rejects anything the Church teaches or practices because he thinks them to be spots, wrinkles or blemishes of the Church blasphemes Christ and His Church.

The Church is the pillar and bulwark of Truth and is infallible.

(I Timothy 3:14-15) *"I am writing these instructions to you so that, if I am delayed, you may know how one ought to behave in the household of God, which is the church of the living God, the pillar and bulwark of the truth."*

A pillar and bulwark is something that holds something else up. In this case, it is the Church who holds up the Truth. If something is not true, then it is a lie. The Church cannot lie. Everything the Church teaches must be true or this passage is meaningless.

"Every one who is of the truth hears my voice."(John 18:37)

"But the hour is coming, and now is, when the true worshipers will worship the Father in spirit and truth, for such the Father seeks to worship him. God is spirit, and those who worship him must worship in spirit and truth."(John 4:23-24)

The worship of the Church is of the spirit and truth. It is not apart from the spirit and truth, or else, it would not be the true Church doing the worshiping.

"[7] Nevertheless I tell you the truth: it is to your advantage that I go away, for if I do not go away, the Counselor will not come to you; but if I go, I will send him to you. [13] When the Spirit of truth comes, he will guide you into all the truth; for he will not speak on his own authority, but whatever he hears he will speak, and he will declare to you the things that are to come."(John 16:7, 13)

"[17] Sanctify them in the truth; thy word is truth. [19] And for their sake I consecrate myself, that they also may be consecrated in truth."(John 17:17, 19)

"And I tell you, you are Peter, and on this rock I will build my church, and the gates of hell shall not prevail against it. I will give you the keys of the kingdom of heaven, and whatever you

bind on earth shall be bound in heaven, and whatever you loose on earth shall be loosed in heaven. "(Matthew 16:18-19)

What are the gates of hell but the lies of the devil and men. If the Church taught one lie, then the powers of hell would prevail. However, Christ promised this never to happen.

The keys are given to one man, Peter. He is that someone whom Christ has given the power and the authority to bind and loose. He is the one whom has been given the authority to anathematize. The keys also denote succession. All this can be seen in (Isaiah 22:22), from which Christ, the Eternal son of David, was drawing from, when He gave Peter the keys, just as Eli'akim was given the key to the house of David.

Therefore, Peter's true successors will have his same power, which ultimately comes from Christ. This has always been the belief and practice of the Church Christ founded.

To reject Peter and his successors' authority is to reject the historic Christian faith and ultimately the Bride of Christ, which is one with Christ. It also means the rejection of the Way, the Truth, and the Life who is Christ himself. Apart from this truth of Peter means apart from salvation. Salvation depends on this truth to make sense of the whole of the Scriptures about what the Church is, does, and means.

Refusing to listen even to the Church, which must by necessity come down to the authority of one man, is to be as the Gentile and tax collector.

"tell it to the church; and if he refuses to listen even to the church, let him be to you as a Gentile and a tax collector. Truly, I say to you, whatever you bind on earth shall be bound in heaven, and whatever you loose on earth shall be loosed in heaven."
(Matthew 18: 17-18)

The Church guards all truth and keeps all false teachings out.

"Abide in me, and I in you. As the branch cannot bear fruit by itself, unless it abides in the vine, neither can you, unless you abide in me. I am the vine, you are the branches. He who abides in me, and I in him, he it is that bears much fruit, for apart from me you can do nothing. If a man does not abide in me, he is cast forth as a branch and withers; and the branches are gathered, thrown into the fire and burned. If you abide in me, and my words abide in you, ask whatever you will, and it shall be done for you. By this my Father is glorified, that you bear much fruit, and so prove to be my disciples. As the Father has loved me, so have I loved you; abide in my love. If you keep my commandments, you will abide in my love, just as I have kept my Father's commandments and abide in his love. "(John 15:4-10)

(Galatians 1:8) *"But even if we, or an angel from heaven, should preach to you a gospel contrary to that which we preached to you, let him be accursed (anathema or cut-off)."*

(I Corinthians 16:21-23) *"I, Paul, write this greeting with my own hand. If any one has no love for the Lord, let him be accursed. Our Lord, come! The grace of the Lord Jesus be with you."*

(II Timothy 4:3-4) *"For the time is coming when people will not endure sound teaching, but having itching ears they will accumulate for themselves teachers to suit their own likings, and will turn away from listening to the truth and wander into myths."*

(I Peter 5:8-9) *"Be sober, be watchful. Your adversary the devil prowls around like a roaring lion, seeking some one to devour. Resist him, firm in your faith"*

(Colossians 1:21-23) *"And you, who once were estranged and hostile in mind, doing evil deeds, he has now reconciled in his body of flesh by his death, in order to present you holy and blameless and irreproachable before him, provided that you continue in the faith, stable and steadfast, not shifting from the hope of the gospel which you heard, which has been preached to every creature under heaven, and of which I, Paul, became a minister."*

(I Timothy 1:3-11) *"As I urged you when I was going to Macedonia, remain at Ephesus that you may charge certain persons not to teach any different doctrine, [4] nor to occupy themselves with myths and endless genealogies which promote speculations rather than the divine training that is in faith; [5] whereas the aim of our charge is love that issues from a pure heart and a good conscience and sincere faith. [6] Certain persons by swerving from these have wandered away into vain discussion, [7] desiring to be teachers of the law, without understanding either what they are saying or the things about which they make assertions. [8] Now we know that the law is good, if any one uses it lawfully, [9] understanding this, that the law is not laid down for the just but for the lawless and disobedient, for the ungodly and sinners, for the unholy and profane, for murderers of fathers and murderers of mothers, for manslayers, [10] immoral persons, sodomites, kidnapers, liars, perjurers, and whatever else is contrary to sound doctrine, [11] in accordance with the glorious gospel of the blessed God with which I have been entrusted."*

(II Tim 1:14) *"guard the truth that has been entrusted to you by the Holy Spirit who dwells within us."*

CONCLUSION

According to the Holy Scriptures, the Church Christ founded is the household of God and Faith. It is a visible institution with divine offices. It has the full authority of Christ to teach, preach, sanctify, and anathematize. The Church is One, Holy, Catholic, and Apostolic. It is united in faith and perfected in truth. Outside this Church, there is no salvation. The Church of Christ can be found in all generations. Only one Church can claim to be this Church for only one has all the marks. One cannot claim to believe in Jesus, the Holy Bible, and Christianity without acknowledging it.

The TRUTH of religion matters for the salvation of men.

Truth is objective. The true religion must be perfect in every way. If one discrepancy can be found by way of doctrine in a particular religion, then the whole religion is corrupt. It must be rejected entirely.

Christ calls man to be perfect. (Matthew 5:48)

If God is to be worshiped in spirit and truth (John 4:24), then a false religion would not be in spirit and truth, but in contradiction and error.

To remain in a false religion as one picks and chooses out of the false religion what is good and what is bad, is not in spirit and truth.

The whole tree must be good. If it bears bad fruit, it should cut down and thrown into the fire. (Luke 3:9, 13:7)

The Vatican 2 Church and all the Protestant, Evangelical, and non-denominational churches are trees that bear nothing but bad fruit, since they all lead to a false relationship with Christ. They all mock Christ and everything that is holy while pretending to be Christian.

In the end, Christ will have them all cut down and thrown into the fire.

Only one Church will be left standing.

The underground Catholic Church, which is the Bride of Christ, will be raised up and brought out of the wilderness (Apoc. 12:6) because she has kept herself pure by not following false doctrine and will be dressed in fine linen (Apoc. 19:7-8), and there will be a great feast.

"And the angel said to me, "Write this: Blessed are those who are invited to the marriage supper of the Lamb." And he said to me, "These are true words of God. "(Apoc. 19:9)

13. THE HISTORY OF THE BAPTIST CHURCHES IN A NUTSHELL

By Steven Speray

April 27, 2006 AD

Living in the Bible belt here in Kentucky for so many years and being surrounded by so many Baptists who have attempted to convert me by way of tracts and booklets has compelled me to give a response using a little history and logic. Since there are so many different types of Baptist churches holding to diverse doctrines and practices, I titled this writing emphasizing the plural churches because the Baptists are not unified in faith. This response will give me the opportunity to use the Baptists as an example showing the importance of knowing your church history.

Today, the Baptist churches have over 25 different branches or sects totaling nearly 32,000,000 members worldwide. The Southern Baptist being the largest body is the largest Protestant organization in the United States.

The name *"Baptist"* comes from the peculiar doctrine of total immersion in baptism conferred only to those who could confess a belief in Christ, which merely symbolized the newfound faith. The Baptists first instituted the doctrine of total immersion of water baptism in 1644, more than 30 years after the first Baptist church was founded.

Contrary to the common myth that Baptists can trace their history back to Christ or John the Baptist, never in history prior to the Reformation do we find an individual or church that claimed the same peculiar beliefs as found in the Baptist churches today. As a matter of fact, the two doctrines (beliefs) shared by all Baptists, total immersion in baptism for adults only as an ordinance, and the *Bible Only* (*Sola Scriptura*) did not exist as beliefs for anyone who claimed Christianity until the 16th and 17th centuries.

Dr. J. M. Carroll's little booklet, *"The Trail of Blood, a History of the Baptist Church,"* gives his account of following the Christians down through the centuries. He also included a chart to better clarify his version of church history. It has sold over 2,000,000 copies and is taught by many Baptists as a factual history of Christianity.

The introduction of this booklet, written by Clarence Walker, begins with a brief history of Dr. Carroll's interest in the history of different denominations, especially their origin. His purpose, of course, was to find the oldest and most like the churches described in the New Testament.

On page 2, a claim is implied that Baptists are not Protestants by referring them separately from the Catholics and Protestants. The map in the back of the booklet clarifies this implication with a statement saying, *"Baptists are not Protestants since they did not come out of the Catholic Church."* In the same paragraph of page 2, another claim is made that Anabaptists existed before the Reformation informing us that Dr. Carroll believes that Anabaptists were the first Baptists.

Since Dr. Carroll is aware that the term Baptists cannot be found in history, he indicates that Baptists came under the nicknames of Anabaptists, Paulicians, Donatists, Albigenses, Waldenses, Montanists, and Novations. (Pages 2, 10, 55)

He states that the Catholic Church put untold numbers of Baptists to death during the dark ages, and goes on to say their history was written in legal documents and papers of those ages.

However, the whole booklet is filled with myths and lies as will be shown next.

The Real History of Baptists

With the corruption of the hierarchy of the Roman Catholic Church, an Augustinian priest named Martin Luther, overreacted in his attack against the corruption of the hierarchy and was then later excommunicated in 1521 for denying the historical understanding of salvation.

In 1517 Germany, during Martin Luther's first attack on the historic Christian doctrines, another preacher named Thomas Munzer attacked Martin Luther's position on how the Church should follow Christ and be saved. Just before his execution in 1525, he recanted everything, made a good confession, received Communion, and died united to the Catholic Church.

Though he maintained Luther's positions on the new doctrines of the *Bible Alone* and *Salvation by Faith Alone*, Munzer also believed the sacrament of baptism to infants was not valid since infants couldn't believe or make a decision in belief. Therefore, his new position was that all babies who were baptized must at the age of reason make a confession of faith and be re-baptized as a sign of the individual's new belief in Christ.

Munzer also denied the sacrament of the Eucharist claiming Christ did not become transubstantiated on the altar of Catholic churches. He believed the Eucharist was merely a symbolic gesture of Christ's sacrifice on the cross. He once undermined the Catholic Mass by using pretzels and beer as meal offerings in place of bread and wine to prove he did not believe in the sacrificial character or the Real Presence. Most Baptists today use crackers and grape juice to indicate the same belief as Munzer.

In 1525, a Catholic priest named Menno Simons set up the first Anabaptist churches. Their purpose was to establish what they held as a spiritual kingdom of converts to real Christianity independent of all civil and church authority. This historic fact debunks Dr. Carroll's contention that Anabaptists existed before the Reformation.

The term Anabaptist or *Re*baptist stems from the fact that these new Protestants practiced rebaptism for all those converted out of the Roman Catholic Church. The rebaptisms always took place with water being poured over the top of the head just as the Roman Catholic Church had been doing for 1500 years. Never was total body immersion thought to be necessary.

Menno Simons' new church came to be known as the Mennonites. The Amish today are one of several sects that have split from the Mennonite Church. They appear to be one and the same to many outside of these two religions.

In 1602, an Anglican priest named John Smyth refusing to conform to the Church of England fled England to Amsterdam, Holland and tried to become a Mennonite. He went so far as to rebaptise himself by pouring water over top of his own head. Again, as an Anglican, he never thought that one needed to be immersed. However, doubting the validity of his self-administered baptism was again rebaptised by the Dutch Mennonites for his third baptism. Due to his views on salvation, the Mennonites later rejected him.

In 1609, he established what we could rightly call the very first Baptist Church in history. In 1611, John Smyth with his friend Thomas Helwys compiled a *"Confession"* or a *"Declaration of Faith"* combining Martin Luther's new doctrines: the Bible alone is the sole authority of faith, and a faith alone for salvation with adult (children but not infants) believers only to be baptized (no mention of immersion as the practice was then of pouring). It also stated the Church must be completely separated from the state. All civil authorities were to take care of temporal affairs only and allow the freedom of religion to all.

The fatal flaws pertaining to these positions is a church constantly dividing, which always comes with a bible only belief, leaving the ultimate interpretation of the Scriptures to each individual. The other is a state that is separated from the Church will always result in an anti-religious state, just as it did in

120

America with its false democratic government which keeps out the reign of Christ as King of its society.

After the death of John Smyth in 1612, Helwys along with his companions returned to England to set up its first Baptist Church at Spitalfields, in London. Thomas Helwys later died in 1616.

The first two churches along with the members were known as the General Baptists for their teaching of the general atonement for all men. They believed in the total free will of man to choose to be saved. Again, they believed in pouring water in baptism until they adopted the method of immersion in 1650 by the splinter group known as the

Immersion Baptists founded in 1644. This group was an offshoot of yet another splinter group called the Particular Baptists founded in the mid 1630's.

It was the Immersion Baptists with their new confession of faith that sealed forever the name that came to be known as the Baptist church. However, they would merge back with the Particular Baptists and become one.

The Particular Baptists founded by John Spillsbury in Southwark, England did not hold to the belief of the general atonement. This group based its beliefs on the new doctrines first founded by the notorious Protestant Reformer John Calvin who claimed a limited (particular) atonement of Christ's sacrifice and along with Luther believed in double-predestination.

Though very Calvinistic at first, they were influenced by the teachings of the Anglican clergymen John and Charles Wesley. With this influence, William Carey in 1792 established missionaries following the example of Roger Williams, the Anglican priest turned Baptist convert who came to America establishing its first Baptist church. He later died rejecting his baptism and organized religion altogether.

In 1891, the Baptist Union of Great Britain and Ireland were formed by a unification of General and Particular Baptists. However, many Baptist churches refused to join in the union, leaving them to be independent churches.

The Baptist churches in America grew quickly and in 1845 divided in three major Conventions: Northern, Southern, and Colored (Black). Later they divided again and again into many different sects. Today there are American Baptists, American Baptists USA, Baptist Bible Fellowship, Missionary Baptists, Bethel Baptists, Central Baptists, Conservative Baptists, Baptist Church of Christ, Free Will Baptists, General Baptists, Landmark Baptists, National Baptists, National Baptists USA, National Missionary Baptists, National Primitive Baptists, North American Baptists, Primitive Baptists, Progressive Baptists, Reformed Baptists, Separate Baptists, Seventh Day Baptists, Southern Baptists, United Baptists, United Free Will Baptists, Berean Fundamental Baptists, Bible Fellowship Baptists, Bible Protestant Baptists, and Bible Way Baptists.

Black Baptists

Since black Americans constitute a large part of Baptists, I would like to touch upon their role in the Baptist religions.

Today, 4 out of 5 blacks in America are Baptists. This is due to the white English Protestants who owned and proselytized their slaves in early America.

The slave trade was justified by the Protestants using the New Testament which speaks of a type of slavery however unlike the slavery of early America. This is the result of Luther's *Bible Only* doctrine, which allows anyone to interpret Scripture entirely for themselves without the authority of the church to put parameters on such interpretations.

The slaves used the Old Testament books showing the horrors of slavery with the example of the captivity of Israel in Egypt. The words of Moses, *"Let my people go"* was the rally cry of slaves who escaped or attempted to escape to freedom from their English slave masters.

Catholics were forbidden to have slaves as all the popes during those times condemned the slave trade as a damnable sin. However, a few so-called Catholics did continue and participate in the slave trade. Most black Catholics in America came from the French who married into the race and the Spanish who helped the slaves escape from the English Protestants.

However, the English greatly outnumbered the French and Spanish and pushed the French to the Southern tip of Louisiana and to the north into Canada, while the Spanish where pushed back into Central and South America.

Though in America most blacks are Baptists, in the rest of the world, black Catholics far outnumber any other religious group for the exception of Islam.

In the mid-1800's, most slaves were Methodists following Wesleyan theology. Over the years the slaves and their children began joining the Baptist churches because of its Calvinist Theology, which is more appealing. Due to the racism found in the churches, blacks began to build and establish their own churches, which they could worship, fellowship, and lead their own congregations.

Contrary to Wesleyan theology, Calvinist theology might stress Christ's words; *"take up my yoke, which is easy"* which concerns resting in Christ for He did all the work and suffering. Not only would this appeal to all men but also especially with slaves who have done nothing but work and suffer their whole lives, not to mention the many years of hardships that followed after their freedom was granted.

For black America today, the Baptist church is the church of family history where the emphasis is on the preaching on Word of God and the praising the Lord in song. The closeness of the black family resides in the faith of their ancestors, which had become the Baptist religions for most of them.

Nicknames of early Baptists?

So what about Dr. Carroll's claim that Baptists came under the nicknames of Paulicians, Anabaptists, Donatists, Albigenses, Waldenses, Montanists, and Novations?

Well, we know about the Anabaptists, but the rest of these groups are a whole other story.

The Paulicians originated from the Eastern Rites of the Catholic Church in the 7th century and continued into the 12th century. They believed Christ only appeared in human form and only seemed to have died. They greatly emphasized the Epistles of Paul (hence the name Paulicians), while rejecting the Epistles of Peter and the entire Old Testament.

Donatists were named after Donatist the Great, a Catholic Bishop of Carthage in 313 AD, who split from the Catholic Church. Donatists were ex-Catholics who believed in all seven sacraments of the Catholic Church. However, they believed the sacraments were invalid if the minister (priest) of the sacraments was impure or in mortal sin. This was contrary to the Catholic belief that Christ is the real minister of the sacraments and the priests were the ambassadors of Christ.

The Montanists originated in the 2nd century and lasted through the 9th century. They believed they were oracles of the Holy Spirit, and the only possessors of any charismatic qualities. They were opposed to any kind of art and were a quasi-form of Gnostics. However, they did believe in the seven sacraments of the Catholic Church.

The Novations were a schismatic group named for the man Novation who set himself up as the pope in 251 AD.

The Albigenses of the 11th century and the Waldenses of the 12th century were a part of Catharism. Cathars had many different sects. In general, they all believed the world and all matter were evil.

Albigenses were named for the place, Albi, France, where the heresy originated. They with the Waldenses were vegetarians who practiced promiscuity. They believed the body was evil and the spirit must be freed from the body. They practiced extreme mortifications with tremendous fasts, sometimes even to the point of suicide. Since they believed offspring was evil, marriage and infant baptism were forbidden. Since they also believed the body was evil, they rejected the incarnation of Christ.

The extreme measure Dr. Carroll goes to prove Baptists go back to the time of Christ is quite an insult to his own religion. For no Baptist would dare claim these groups as their own who rejected the Old Testament and the Epistles of Peter, believed in the seven sacraments of the Catholic Church, and forbidding marriage while practicing promiscuity.

However, the attempt to find the oldest and most like the church described in the New Testament is made by Dr. Carroll because he realized it is absolutely necessary to demonstrate their church or at least their beliefs can be found and substantiated in every generation since Christ.

Unfortunately for them, only one church can do what they wish their church could do. The Roman Catholic Church is the only church found in every generation since Christ and has always remained unified in doctrine resulting in a unified Church. Only the Catholic Church can be totally substantiated in history, Scripture and logic.

As for the untold numbers of Baptists who were put to death by the Catholic Church during the dark ages, they were untold because it didn't happen. As for their history being written in legal documents and papers of those ages, they don't exist and never did. Dr. Carroll just plain lied about it because he knew the biggest obstacle in his belief system was the Roman Catholic Church. Thankfully, however, rumor has it that he recanted everything on his deathbed and admitted his lies.

As for the claim that Baptists were not Protestants since they did not come out of the Catholic Church is a half-truth since they actually came out of the Church of England under the influence of the Dutch Mennonites. This means that they were Protestants since they held to the two foundational doctrines never known in history, which caused the revolt against Rome.

Conclusion

The common thread for all Baptists is the practice of adult baptism by total immersion only while rejecting infant baptism. All Baptists believe in Luther's doctrine of *Sola Scriptura* or the *Bible Only* as the sole authority on faith. All Baptists agree with Luther, Calvin, and the other notorious Reformers that the Catholic Church's papacy is false because Protestants believe it is unbiblical in their personal interpretations of the Scripture, which again stems from the doctrine of *Sola Scriptura*.

Most Baptists believe in Luther and Calvin's doctrine once-saved-always-saved.

With this in mind, Catholics have five important questions for Baptists:

1. What church would you have attended before the first Baptist church was established and built in 1609 or before the Protestant Revolt?

2. If you already know for sure you are going to be in heaven, why the need to hope and work out your salvation in fear and trembling as St Paul said to do? After all, if you know already you're going to heaven, hope is not needed, and there would be no need to fear and tremble.

3. In light of St. Paul stating in a salvation context that he might end up a reprobate himself if he didn't buffet his body, how is it he didn't know for sure he was going to heaven but you do?

4. If once saved always saved is true, why does the Bible warn in a salvation context of falling away or being cut off if it were impossible for one to fall away or be cut off?

5. Why belong to a man-made religion based on man-made beliefs about the Bible, which run contrary to the entire 1500-year history of Christianity? If the answer is something like, *"My beliefs come from the Bible"*then what about the entire Christian world who never believed in those things for next 1500 years until those particular beliefs were resurrected during the 16th century?

Since the Baptist churches are not united in their interpretation of Scripture, they claim that it doesn't really matter what church of faith you belong to as long as you believe and trust Jesus.

However, did not Christ pray that they (the church) be one? Did Christ's prayer fail to achieve what He asked the Father? Did not Christ say that the gates of hell would never prevail against his church?

Doesn't that mean His church is to be found in every generation till the end of time teaching nothing but the truth?

History is the key.

We are told to hold fast to the faith that was delivered from the beginning and calls to mind the warning of St. Paul, *"But even if we, or an angel from heaven, should preach to you a gospel contrary to that which we preached to you, let him be accursed. As we have said before, so now I say again, If any one is preaching to you a gospel contrary to that which you received, let him be accursed."*Galatians 1:8-9

The Baptist Church's interpretation of Scripture was never believed or taught for 1500 years of Christianity such as the Bible being the ONLY authority and rule of faith, or adult baptism by immersion only, or a once-saved-always-saved belief.

The historic Christian recognizes that the Baptist faith is another gospel, which was never ever preached by anyone until the 16th century Protestant Revolt. According to St. Paul under the inspiration of the Holy Spirit, *"let him be accursed."*

When Baptist preachers are confronted with this contradiction, they almost always retort that it is not about religion but a relationship.

This final statement is all they can muster because in the end they know their religion could not be truly and logically justified historically or even by Holy Scripture. It doesn't matter to them because they claim to have a relationship with Christ and nothing was going to separate that relationship.

The problem with this understanding is religion is the very substance of the relationship. Without the religion, the relationship is hollow. The very definition of religion is the system of belief based on faith and the outward practices of life by which men indicate their relationship with God.

This means that a false religion is a false relationship with one's own God or a wrong religion is a wrong relationship with one's own God.

It's that simple.

Christ instituted the Catholic Church so we can have the right relationship with Him. Those who refuse to accept it are like the ones whom Jesus spoke, *"He who rejects you rejects me and he who rejects me rejects the one who sent me."*

There are many people who completely fabricate lies about the Catholic Church, and/or misrepresent it.

I've seen it all and it amazes me how easy it is to debunk them all.

Christ said, *"The path to destruction is a wide one and many are those who take it, but the path to paradise is a narrow one and few who even find it."* We may live in a confusing world but the narrow path can be found for Christ would not have left us without being able to find it.

I submit the Catholic Faith is that path for it is the only faith that can be found throughout the entire history of Christianity. It was the faith of Peter to whom Jesus gave the keys. It was the faith of all Peter's successors. It was the faith of Stephen who was the first to die because of it. It was the faith of all the saints.

The Roman Catholic Faith is the faith found in all generations since Christ and if this faith is not it... then nothing else is.

www.ingramcontent.com/pod-product-compliance
Lightning Source LLC
Chambersburg PA
CBHW032151020726
47496CB00003B/825